The Birth of Greek Civilization

The
Birth of Greek
Civilization

Pavel Oliva

BOOK CLUB ASSOCIATES
LONDON

The publishers would like to thank the following
for providing the illustrations on the pages listed below:
British Museum 98, 102 top, 168 bottom;
Peter Clayton 51; Colin Grant 53 left, 161;
Hirmer Fotoarchiv 50, 99, 102 bottom left, 102 bottom right, 104,
162-3, 167 top, 167 bottom, 168 top; IGDA 164 right;
Mansell Collection 49, 52 top, 56, 100, 103, 164 left, 165, 166;
Scala 54 bottom, 101, 163 bottom;
Ronald Sheridan 53 right, 54 top, 55.

Translated by Iris Urwin Levitová

This edition published 1981 by Book Club Associates

By arrangement with Orbis Publishing

© 1981 by Orbis Publishing Limited, London
First published in Great Britain by Orbis Publishing Limited,
London 1981

Printed in Great Britain
by Morrison and Gibb Ltd, Edinburgh
ISBN 0-85613-321-3

Contents

CHAPTER I

From Early
Neolithic Times to the Height
of the Bronze Age

Greek tradition kept alive an awareness of the 'heroic age'. Myths, most explicit in epic poetry and in drama, portrayed the fates of the powerful Mycenaean kings, the dramatic events in Boeotian Thebes, the famous expedition of the Achaean warriors to the walls of Troy in Asia Minor, the Argonauts setting out from Iolcus in Thessaly for Colchis on the shores of the Black Sea, and the labyrinth on Crete, said to have been built for King Minos in Knossos by the Athenian Daedalus.

Greek historians did not draw a clear line between this mythical past and the attested events of history. Herodotus relates that the Trojan War broke out 'in the third generation after the death of Minos' (7,171). For him it was unquestionably a historical event, as was Jason's expedition to Colchis to bring back the Golden Fleece (1,2–3; 7,193). Even so rational a historian as Thucydides opened his account of the earliest history of the Greeks with a reference to Minos (1,4). Although he was aware that Homer's verse dates from a period much later than that in which the events surrounding the fall of Troy are supposed to have happened (1,3,3), he does not doubt the historical authenticity of the poet, or of Agamemnon, King of Mycenae (1,9). Later writers of antiquity, too, accepted as reliable the accounts handed down in myths. The Hellenistic polyhistorian Eratosthenes of Cyrene, who introduced a systematic chronology based on the Olympic Games, began his survey of historical events in Greece with the fall of Troy, which he dated to 1184/3 BC. Other writers on history and chronology attribute the fall of Troy to various dates from the 1330s to the 1130s BC, a difference of two centuries.

Modern historians have naturally taken a critical stand on 'facts' drawn from Greek mythology, and have refused to accept the heroic age as historical. One of the founders of Greek historical studies, the English writer George Grote, in the middle of the last century, distinguished between myth and history proper, which he thought began when the Olympic Games were instituted, i.e. 776 BC.

Not long afterwards, however, the sources for Greek history began to expand to a surprising degree. A new scholarly discipline, archaeology, was responsible. After the first modest beginnings at Cnidus in Asia Minor and Eleusis in Attica during the 1850s, there came the epoch-making discoveries connected with the name of the 'enthusiastic amateur' Heinrich Schliemann. His excavations of the site of Troy and Mycenae in the 1870s, literally with a copy of Homer's *Iliad* in his hand, revealed to the astonished eyes of historians and philologists that heroic Greece had actually once existed. It did not matter that the Trojan 'Priam's Treasure' was found in a stratum (II) which probably dates from as far back as the third quarter of the third millennium, and is thus more than a thousand years older than the 'traditional' date for the Trojan War, nor that the gold 'mask of Agamemnon' from Mycenae lay in a grave now dated to the sixteenth century BC. Archaeological investigation in the region of the Aegean took another significant step forward when Evans made his discoveries at Knossos, on the island of Crete, in the first decades of our own century, and revealed the reality behind the myths of Minos and his labyrinth.

Archaeological excavation of settlements not only of these early eras, but also of other fully historical periods of Greek antiquity, in many cases found not only the material remains they expected, but also evidence of even earlier phases than Minoan Crete and Mycenaean Greece. Signs of prehistoric cultures were found in Thessaly and at some places in central Greece, on Crete and in the Peloponnese. In time not only the Bronze Age and the world of antiquity were opened up to study, but the Greek Neolithic Age as well. Similar developments were taking place elsewhere in the Aegean and in the Middle East, where earlier Neolithic cultures have been discovered alongside the mature civilizations of Mesopotamia, Syria, Palestine, Egypt, and Asia Minor. Since the Second World War, specialization and new techniques have led to astounding results. Certain discoveries in the natural sciences have been turned to good account in archaeology, particularly the use of radioactive carbon isotopes for dating, discovered in 1949 by the American physicist W. F. Libby. This method is based on the discovery that all organic matter contains radioactive carbon isotopes (Carbon-14) which gradually turn to ordinary carbon (Carbon-12) after the matter dies. Since we know the half-life of the C-14 isotope (according to the latest calculations it is about 5,730 years), it is possible to determine the age of the organic matter excavated, and thus the age of the archaeological horizon in which it was found. There are various factors which prevent results from being reliable in every case, and it is usual to allow a margin of a few dozen years at least. Nevertheless this method, and the technique known as dendro-chronology, based on the number of rings in the wood of ancient trees, have much improved our ability to date prehistoric cultures.

Man began to settle down and his numbers to increase when he became a herdsman and farmer, a phenomenon which dates from the transition from the Middle Stone Age (Mesolithic Age) to the Late Stone Age (Neolithic). People already knew how to make fairly efficient tools and weapons, including sickles with which to gather grain crops, and mills in which to crush the grain for flour. Grain could be found growing wild over a vast area stretching from the western foothills of the Himalayas to the eastern Mediterranean. This area also fed goats, sheep and cattle, species very suitable for breeding. The beginning of the Neolithic Age used to be linked to discoveries of pottery vessels, an important sign of settled habitation, but more recent research has shown that in many places the beginnings of herding and farming, marking the opening of the Neolithic Age, can be dated far earlier than the occurrence of pottery. The name aceramic Neolithic is therefore given to this early phase of the Neolithic Age.

The transition from food-gathering to food producing was a long process. Particularly favourable conditions were to be found among foothills, where there was sufficient rainfall and fertile soil. The oldest evidence of this early Neolithic (Proto-Neolithic) Age has been found in the foothills of the Zagros range in Iraqi Kurdistan. The finds from Shanidar Cave and the nearby hamlet of Zawi Chemi date from the end of the tenth and the first half of the ninth millennium BC. At the turn of the eighth millennium there were several Neolithic settlements in the Iranian and Iraqi foothills of the Zagros range. Early Neolithic settlements are also known in Palestine (Jericho) and important finds have been made in Asia Minor in the last twenty years, among them an excavated settlement at Hacılar on the south-west fringe of the Taurus Mountains, where the aceramic phase began at the end of the eighth and the beginning of the seventh millennia, and the excavations at Çatal Hüyük in the plateau north of the Taurus. At the latter site the Neolithic settlement can be dated between 7100 and 6300 BC, and its extent and the relatively high technical skills revealed make it one of the earliest known settlements of an urban type; the sophisticated architecture includes shrines decorated with coloured relief carvings and paintings, and there are numerous useful articles and works of art. There is evidence, too, of a cult of the fertility goddess.

From these oldest centres the Neolithic culture spread very far. Impulses emerging from Kurdistan spread over the Iranian plateau and the southern reaches of Central Asia, and found particularly favourable conditions in Mesopotamia. Influences from Asia Minor led to the flowering of settlements in Syria (Ras Shamra) and spread further west, to the Balkan peninsula.

In recent years evidence of Palaeolithic settlement in Greece has been uncovered, much of it in Thessaly particularly from the valley of the Peneus; the find of a Neanderthal skull from the peninsula of Chalcidice is part of this evidence. Palaeolithic industry is attested from other parts of Greece, as well, and from what we know today we can safely assume that there were hunters in northern and central Greece (and perhaps in the north-east part of the Peloponnese as well) as early as the Middle Palaeolithic Age. Traces of Mesolithic settlement have also been found both on the mainland and on some islands.

The oldest evidence of Early Neolithic settlement on Greek territory appears to date from the seventh millennium BC. Three aceramic Neolithic settlements have been found in Thessaly (the lower level of Sesklo, Argissa and Souphli-Magula). As in the Near East, stone sickle blades and grain crushers have been found. The people in these settlements lived by primitive agriculture and raised stock, primarily sheep. The general standard seems to have been lower than that of similar sites in the east, however; the architecture is more primitive and no stone vessels or cult statuettes have been found.

The aceramic phase of the Neolithic Age was followed, at least in some places, by the Neolithic phase characterized by pottery. It is not possible to prove continuity between the two phases, however, or to assume that it was a native Greek development. It is highly probable that the bearers of this new and more mature Neolithic culture were once more immigrants from the east. Certain analogies in the ceramic products suggest that they may have come from the region of Çatal-Hüyük.

The ceramic Neolithic culture probably evolved in Greece from the beginning of the sixth millennium, and formed a long era right up to the beginning of the third millennium BC. It covered a greater area than the aceramic Neolithic culture, and has been attested in Sesklo, Argissa and other places in Thessaly as well as in central Greece (Elateia in Phocis, Nea Macri on the eastern coast of Attica) and the north-eastern Peloponnese (Corinth, Lerna). An important Early Neolithic settlement has also been found in Macedonia, at Nea Nicomedeia (now northern Greece). One surprising result of a single

11

Carbon-14 dating, which needs to be supported by other evidence, is the suggestion that the settlement dates from the last quarter of the seventh millennium BC.

Like the Neolithic settlements in the Near East, those in Greece offer a variety of small animal figurines and statuettes of steatopygous (fat-buttocked) women, testifying to a cult of the goddess of fertility. Clay seals are rarer, and stone seals an exceptional find. The earliest pottery is not decorated, and it took a long time (about 400 years in Elateia, it has been calculated) before the first decorated pottery appeared. There were many variants developed, differing both in shape and in decoration. In Thessaly, for example, the earliest plain pottery was followed by a phase called after the principal site, the Proto-Sesklo phase. Towards the end of the Early Neolithic period a new type of pottery appears, and has been given the name Pre-Sesklo. Pottery decorated with regular incisions also appeared, perhaps originating in the northern Balkans. A different type of clay pot, for which analogies can be found in south-east Asia Minor, occurs on the Nea Macri site.

During the Middle Neolithic period the differences between various regions of the Greek mainland became more profound. The culture we know as Sesklo predominated in Thessaly, brought by new arrivals from the east. A characteristic feature of the Sesklo culture was the square courtyard built on stone foundations, with columns within. This gradually developed into the *megaron*, the typical architectural form for Greece in later ages too. The pottery of this period shows the influence of the Samarra culture, named after a Neolithic settlement in the middle reaches of the Tigris valley. From here the Samarra culture spread over a vast area stretching from the upper Euphrates in the north-west to the fringes of the Iranian plateau in the south-east, in the second half of the sixth millennium BC. In addition to geometrical ornament this pottery is decorated with stylized plant, animal and human motifs, and there is a clear attempt to portray motion. These new elements were probably brought to Thessaly by a new wave of immigrants from Asia Minor or even from northern Mesopotamia.

In the more southern parts of Greece the Middle Neolithic period developed quite differently. In Phocis and Boeotia elements of the Early Neolithic culture went on evolving, but in the Peloponnese and some other parts of central Greece we find the influence of the early phase of an important eastern culture known as the Halaf culture, from the site at Tell Halaf (now eastern Syria). The products of this culture at its height, known mainly from the upper Tigris valley, are among the most sophisticated examples of Neolithic culture.

The Late Neolithic period was characterized in Greece by the forging of links between the different regions, so long cut off from each other. In eastern Thessaly the culture known as Dhimini, from the most important site, thrived; it had evolved from the Sesklo culture, but the influence of the Cyclades islands can be traced too. The settlement of Dhimini itself was fortified with several concentric walls. During this final phase of Neolithic culture, as in earlier periods, Greece was influenced by the more mature cultures of the Near East.

In Crete developments were quite distinct. A number of sites yielding Neolithic material have been found, but this is almost exclusively from the Late Neolithic period. The only exception to date is Knossos, where a deep layer of Neolithic was found. The chronology of the Neolithic Age in Crete is uncertain. The earliest Neolithic pottery found in Knossos dates from about the middle of the fifth millennium BC, but traces have been found of an older, aceramic phase which can be dated to the turn of the seventh millennium. There is no continuity between these two phases, and so we must assume that evolution here was interrupted for a long period. Analogous finds to those on the Greek mainland date from the Late Neolithic period in Knossos, too.

Metal-working, especially copper, is very ancient. In the Iranian Neolithic settlement of Tepe Sialk, for instance, copper awls and pins were found, hammered from cold metal, and dating from the sixth millennium; in the fifth millennium copper axes and punches were in use. Much evidence of metal-working has been discovered in the region of the Halaf culture and there were three Chalcolithic centres in Asia Minor at the end of the sixth millennium. Remarkable finds were made in Çatal-Hüyük, including ornaments of copper and lead foil dating from as early as the middle of the seventh millennium. Copper was in use in Late Neolithic times in Greece and Crete, too. It was the discovery of bronze, however, a firm alloy of tin and copper, that changed the character of tools and weapons, although this did not mean, of course, that stone and bone were no longer used as materials.

In Greece the Bronze Age, known on the mainland as the Helladic culture, can be said to have begun in the second quarter of the third millennium. Finds attesting this new culture, which was also characterized by new types of pottery, come from Boeotia and other parts of central Greece, including the eastern shores of Attica. Many sites have been discovered in the north-east Peloponnese as well, including such important centres of Mycenaean civilization as Tiryns and Asine, and especially Lerna, already known as an Early and Middle Neolithic site.

In the Early Bronze Age in the Aegean the Cyclades played a significant role. These rocky islands lying off the coast of Attica and Euboea to the north, towards Rhodes and the mainland of Asia Minor to the south-east, and towards Crete to the south, were probably settled permanently from the end of the Neolithic Age. Their small bays offered safe harbours for the boats of the day, the sea made contacts easy and land was rarely out of sight. The Cyclades provided a source of obsidian, the black glassy stone formed by rapidly cooling volcanic lava. Melos was particularly rich in deposits of obsidian, which could be used for hard blades and the tips of tools and weapons. The Cyclades, especially Paros and Naxos, were later famed for their good quality marble. The mining of gold and silver in the Cyclades may have dated from this period, too, for vessels of precious metal of quite early date have been found here.

A characteristic feature of Early Cycladic culture, probably developing from the early third millennium, were the marble statuettes, mostly female figures. These figurines were not the steatopygous fertility goddesses known to us from Neolithic and in fact from Late Palaeolithic cultures; the sexual and fertility traits were not exaggerated. Most of the figures are slender, standing with the head inclined and the hands folded loosely over the abdomen or hanging by their sides. The head and the different parts of the body are not skilfully modelled, and yet they show an artistic sense for abstract expression. The figures are usually described as idols, and they appear to be part of a cult and a system of religious ideas of which we have no knowledge. Male figures are rarely found, and usually represented musicians playing the double pipe or the harp. Cycladean statuettes have been found in Crete and on the Greek mainland, as imports.

Cycladean pottery was not turned on the wheel in the Early or the Middle Bronze Age, nor was the local clay particularly suitable for the purpose. Spirals and circles were often used as ornamentation and were used either incised or impressed, using stamps. Clay 'pans' were a particularly interesting item; they were probably used for toilet purposes, but the ornamentation, which emphasizes fertility symbols, suggests that they may have had some magical function as well.

For metropolitan Greece the beginning of the Early Bronze Age (Early Helladic) is usually dated to the second third of the third millennium. A considerable number of Early Helladic sites have been found, particularly in Thessaly, east central Greece and the Peloponnese. Since the Second World War the settlement at Eutresis in Boeotia (to the west of Thebes) in central Greece has been carefully investigated; the Early Helladic settlement was preceded by a Middle Neolithic and a Late Neolithic settlement. Recently attention has been focused on Lerna in Argolis, in the north-east of the Peloponnese; there were settlements here in Early and in Middle Neolithic times, and then again in the Early Helladic period. It is not without interest that the locality has its place in Greek mythology: one of the twelve tasks imposed upon Heracles was that of killing the terrible hydra which had its home in the marshes around Lerna.

There was a surprising discovery in Lerna, where destruction at the end of the second phase of the Early Helladic period (EH II) was succeeded by a period (EH III) marked by quite distinct cultural elements. These include grey pottery remarkably similar to pottery in other Greek localities of the Middle Helladic phase. The pottery found in Lerna is a coarser ware, however. As this pottery, which imitates the appearance of metal vessels, was discovered in Boeotian Orchomenus, where the mythical King Minyas ruled, it has come to be known as Minyan ware.

Earlier scholars linked the new cultural elements, including Minyan ware in a significant place, with the arrival of a new ethnic group in mainland Greece, who were considered the Greeks proper. This meant that the Greek people were thought to have reached their new homeland at the beginning of the Middle Helladic period, that is to say about the year 1900 BC. The Lerna finds suggest that these events were already taking place in the preceding period (EH III), and must be dated about two centuries earlier (c.2100 BC). The situation was further complicated by the discovery of grey ware of the Minyan type in north-west Asia Minor. Some scholars link these examples of the material culture with the Indo-European Luwians (related to the Hittites) and suggest that these were the people who brought the Minyan ware to the Greek mainland; this would mean that Luwian settlement preceded settlement of the mainland by the Greeks. Linguistic arguments have been brought in to support this view, based on certain types of topographical names in Greece. Yet another school of thought has the ancestors of the later Greeks moving from the northern Balkans into Asia Minor, and only then arriving back in Greece.

Discoveries will undoubtedly be made which will throw new light on the involved question of when the Greek tribes arrived in what was to become their homeland. Leaving aside the extreme views of those who reject the interpretation of the earliest written records on the Greek mainland, and who date the arrival of the Greeks there to after the fall of the Mycenaean civilization, it must be admitted that Greek settlement is reliably attested during the Late Helladic (Mycenaean) period. Since, however, the archaeological material shows no break in continuity between Middle and Late Helladic, one can assume that the forerunners of the Greeks were already present at the beginning of the second millennium, or even, as the Lerna finds suggest, towards the end of the third millennium. We have no idea what their relations with the earlier inhabitants of the Greek mainland may have been. It is possible that violent invasion was followed by gradual infiltration by succeeding waves of immigrants, which would have strengthened the Greek (or, to be more exact, the proto-Greek) ethnic group.

During the Middle Bronze Age the centre of developments in Aegean culture shifted from the Cyclades to Crete. In what is known as the pre-palace culture (Early Minoan), probably beginning in the third quarter of the third millennium, we already find evidence of contacts between Crete and her more sophisticated neighbours in the world of antiquity. Pottery finds from the eastern part of the island show affinities with pottery from Asia Minor. Relations with Egypt were lively, Cretan craftsmen acquiring skill in the making of stone vessels and the firing of a special pottery with a glass-like finish, known as faience. Seals, especially stamp seals, came from Egypt to Crete, where cylindrical seals of the traditional form known in the Near East were rare. The Cretans were also influenced by ideas from the Greek mainland, and particularly from the Cyclades. During the last phase of the pre-palace culture it was from the Cyclades that marble 'idols' reached Crete, where they soon found imitators. The Cycladean spiral motif also became popular in decorating Cretan pottery.

Since the first palaces were discovered in Crete early in the twentieth century by Sir Arthur Evans and others, recent literature describes the first two phases of the Middle Minoan period (Evans' periodization) as the period of the older palaces; in absolute chronology this is c. 2000–1700 BC. Besides Knossos itself, which was already the most important site in Crete in Neolithic times, palaces were built in Phaestus in southern Crete and in Mallia, east of Knossos.

In Crete, as in the Near East, the palace was not only the residence of the ruler and the seat of the central administration, but also the economic centre for quite a large area. As a rule the crafts were concentrated there, while capacious warehouses were used to store agricultural products, especially grain, wine and olive oil. The palace also ran its own large herds of cattle, sheep, pigs and goats. The storage capacity of the palace at Knossos was greater than that of the palaces excavated in Mesopotamia, Syria, or Egypt, but there are considerable differences of plan. In the Near East the outer walls of the palace were what determined the plan of the palace, which had to be safe from enemy attack. In Crete the palace buildings were arranged round a spacious courtyard, and there were no fortifying walls. The palaces were built a few kilometres from the sea, within easy reach of the harbour but not close enough to risk sudden attack from the sea. There do not seem to have been conflicts between the rulers of the different palaces in Crete.

During the period of the older palaces, excellent pottery was produced in Knossos and in Phaestus. The first finds were made in the cave shrine of the village of Kamares, in the range of Mount Ida, and so it became known as Kamares ware. Made on a potter's wheel, these vessels are thin-walled, of perfect shape and bright ornament using motifs from nature. In Kamares ware the Cretan art of vase painting reached its highest point, only surpassed by the workshops of archaic Greece. It was exported to Egypt. Cretan spiral ornament appears in the rock tombs of the Twelfth Dynasty in Egypt, and the influence of Cretan craftsmen can be seen in the work of Egyptian goldsmiths. Timber, especially cypress, was exported to Egypt from Crete, while from Egypt came luxury articles and the ivory, gold and precious stones the Cretan jewellers and goldsmiths needed for their art. The Cretan ships maintained active contact with the Greek mainland, especially with Lerna, and with the islands in the Aegean. Towards the east Crete carried on trade with Cyprus and probably through Cyprus with Ugarit (Ras Shamra) in Syria, and even further on, with Mari.

The administration of such a palace economy involved careful keeping of records, and we find written records in Crete as early as the beginning of the Middle Minoan period. A unique script was developed, a picture-writing which is sometimes called hieroglyphic, purely on analogy with the Egyptian script, but more often called pictographic. The earliest use of these signs is on seals: very few inscriptions on tablets and clay fragments have survived, and the individual records are all very slight in extent. Apart from the probable identity of a certain number of ideograms (characters expressing abstract concepts), all that has been deciphered so far are the signs for numbers; it is clear that the Cretans used a decadic system. The pictographic script was syllabic in character and remained in use until about the middle of the seventeenth century BC.

In addition to the pictographic script, what is known as Linear A was also used in the older palace period; this is also a syllabic script and may have been based on the pictographic one. The simpler linear signs were more suitable for recording than the pictorial signs of the pictographic script. Records in Linear A script have been preserved mainly on clay tablets, on walls and on ritual articles, but their number is few. After the later Linear B script had been deciphered, many signs being closely similar to signs in Linear A, it was possible to work out the probable phonetic expression of these signs. But no attempts have as yet succeeded in determining the language of Linear A, which is unlikely to belong either to the Indo-European or the Semitic group.

The older palaces were destroyed about the year 1700 BC, probably by an earthquake. They were restored soon afterwards, however, and Knossos and Phaestus in particular saw a new era of prosperity. This was the period of the new palaces, the first phase of which corresponds to Evans' third stage of the Middle Minoan period; in absolute chronology this period covers most of the seventeenth and about the first two decades of the sixteenth century BC. At this time Crete was becoming more important in the Aegean, and marked signs of Minoan influence can be seen on Cythera, on Thera, Melos and Ceos, Aegina, Rhodes, and at Miletus in Asia Minor. In later Greek accounts the penetration of the mature Cretan culture to other parts of the Aegean is seen as the expression of Minoan thalassocracy (dominion over the sea). Just as King Minos of Knossos was a mythical figure, so was the dominion of Knossos over the Aegean no more than a poetical fiction. The influence of Crete was felt primarily in commercial and cultural contacts, and was not in the nature of political power.

Contact between Crete and Egypt continued, and one of the forms it took was the mutual exchange of certain elements in mural painting. Cretan faience work dates from this period, too, especially the famous figures of goddesses (or perhaps priestesses) brandishing snakes.

The famous Phaestus Disk was probably fashioned about the year 1600 BC; this disk of baked clay found in the palace at Phaestus is covered on both sides with pictorial signs quite distinct from the pictographic script of Crete. The pictograms were impressed on the clay with dies of some hard material, before the disk was fired. Some scholars are of the opinion that the Phaestus Disk comes from the south-west of Asia Minor (later to become Lycia) where several similar pictograms have been found, but it is not impossible that the disk originated in Crete.

At the beginning of the sixteenth century BC, perhaps around 1580, catastrophe fell on Crete, probably again caused by an earthquake. It is possible that this natural calamity was followed by destruction at the hands of enemies, yet once again the damage was not irreparable.

During the century from about 1570 BC (or according to some writers, from 1550), Minoan civilization attained its greatest glory. This late palace phase is roughly equal to the first stage of the Late Minoan period. It was the time when the Mycenaean (Late Helladic) civilization was emerging on the Greek mainland, and at least for a time superseded Cretan contacts with Egypt. For most of the sixteenth century Egypt seems to have imported only Mycenaean wares, and Cretan goods appeared again only towards the end of the century. Besides Knossos and Phaestus, the palace at Mallia grew in importance; and at Phaestus the ruler built a royal 'villa' for himself as well, not far from the palace and now known as Hagia Triada from the chapel of the Holy Trinity in the vicinity. Another prospering palace economy, excavated in the first half of the 1960s, was that near the village of (Kato) Zacros in eastern Crete.

Many remarkable works of art have been found, dating from this peak period of Minoan civilization. Vessels of soft stone carved in low relief were very popular. An interesting vase was found in Hagia Triada; known as the Harvesters' Vase, it shows a procession of twenty-seven figures, but it is more likely that it portrays a sowing rather than a harvesting celebration.

From the sixteenth and fifteenth centuries we have bronze objects worked with the *cire perdue* technique; typical figures present men and women with the right hand raised to the brow in a gesture of adoration. Large numbers of Cretan *objets d'art* have been found on the Greek mainland, two of the most important being gold chalices with scenes depicting a wild bull hunt in *repoussé*. They came from a tomb at Vaphio, not far from Sparta.

Mural painting was a highlight of Cretan art at this period. The frescoes, best preserved in the palace at Knossos, often depicted scenes from nature, realistic studies of animals, birds and flowers (like the famous blue monkey in a field of saffron) as well as marine creatures (fish and dolphins). The scenes of daily life in the palace, depicting religious rites, festivities, dances and acrobatic feats with bulls, are of documentary value for what they tell us of the nature of Minoan life. We have the portraits of noble men and especially of 'court ladies' in fashionable luxury. We see the audience as well as the actors in religious rites and games. A unique work of art from the world of antiquity is the miniature fresco from Knossos, portraying not only a group of dancing girls, but hundreds of people sitting among the olive trees and watching the dance. Mural painting was also well developed in the Cyclades, as can be seen from the Melos finds, and especially from the masterpieces among the frescoes on Thera, discovered some years ago and now exhibited in the National Archaeological Museum, Athens.

The Late Minoan vases found in 1866 under layers of volcanic ash on Thera, even before Schliemann discovered Troy and ten years earlier than his excavations at Mycenae, are among the earliest examples of a mature Bronze Age culture in the Aegean. Excavations were begun on Thera at the end of the last century, before Evans had made his discoveries on Crete, but work was made very difficult by the deposits of volcanic ash and lava, and it was not until modern technical devices could be used that success came in the course of the systematic investigation of the site started by the Greek archaeologist S. Marinatos in 1967.

The eruption of the volcano on Thera was one of the greatest disasters known in the region of the Aegean, and its consequences were enormous. A large part of the island sank into the sea, and what remained was covered deep in ash and lava. Volcanic activity has been repeated more than once in the area, the last time being in the 1920s. Scholars vary in their dating of the catastrophic eruption in the middle of the second millennium BC, and some writers assume that there were two or even three such disasters. It is perhaps likely that after the first earthquake about the year 1520 BC there was an eruption some fifty years later which completely changed the contours of the island and sent a tidal wave to the northern shores of Crete, where great damage was done. It may be that this catastrophe is mirrored in the ancient legend of the destruction of Atlantis, told by the Egyptian priest to Solon in Plato's *Timaeus*.

It was probably in consequence of the natural catastrophe that befell Thera and some other islands, including Crete, that there was a marked change in the trend of Minoan civilization. From the middle of the fifteenth century, or perhaps already from the seventies, the domination of Knossos on the island was strengthened, and Mallia, Phaestus and other localities seem to have come under the central rule of Knossos. Although the material culture of Crete remained Minoan in character, some of the pottery and weapons found in warriors' tombs show influence which must have come from the Greek mainland. The suggestion that at this period it was Greek (Achaean) aristocrats who ruled from Knossos was further strengthened by the deciphering of Linear B script.

After many attempts had failed, a British architect, Michael Ventris, tackled the problem by using mathematical statistics in a method of combinations, in 1952, assisted at the final stage by a linguist, John Chadwick. The discovery by Ventris that the records in Linear B script are in the Greek language is in substance generally accepted today, in spite of some opposition.

Nevertheless it is difficult to interpret the surviving texts. The clay tablets are often in a very bad state of preservation, and frequently in fragments; they are often hardly legible. The linear syllabic script which was not originally developed for Greek does not give the exact phonetic form of the word (in some cases the consonants are not signalized). The language used in Linear B texts is several centuries older than the Greek we know from the earliest monuments of archaic Greece. Detailed analysis has shown that the Greek used on the Knossos tablets, like that on Linear B tablets found in Mycenaean Greece, is closest to the dialects of Arcadia and Cyprus at a later period, and partly to the Aeolic dialect. For the most part the records are brief and refer to palace and ritual business. It is difficult to put the odd scraps of information into a context which was so obvious to the scribes that they did not bother to note it down.

These clay tablets were not fired, and so only those tablets have survived which were stored in the palace at the time of the great fire. This probably destroyed the palace at Knossos at the beginning of the fourteenth century BC, and it was not rebuilt. In the post-palace period, corresponding to the third stage of the Late Minoan period and covering most of the fourteenth and all the thirteenth century, Mycenaean influences became much stronger in Crete. It was mainly in the religious sphere that Minoan traditions persisted.

From the remains of material culture and the written records of the last phase of the Minoan civilization it is clear that the type of state which had developed in Crete was similar to contemporary states in the Near East. Supreme power rested with the ruler of the palace, but the court aristocracy played an important part. In the close neighbourhood of the palace at Knossos elegant houses were excavated, obviously belonging to this upper class. Large numbers of artists and craftsmen worked in the palace; pottery, stone-working and weaving shops have been found. Archaeological investigation on

Crete has revealed urban-type settlements as well as the palace. The most extensive such settlement was at Gournia in the north-east of the island, where narrow streets of little houses were occupied by artisans, fishermen and sailors, as well as by those working on the land. There can be no doubt that large numbers were engaged in agriculture and tending the herds. The Knossos tablets include numerous records of sheep husbandry; the number of sheep registered as kept for their wool was over a hundred thousand head. Wool was one of the primary sources of wealth for the rulers of Knossos, and a stable article of trade, which remained at the level of barter.

No temples have been found in Minoan Crete; religious ritual centred on the mountain peaks, caves and sacred trees, but ceremonies mostly took place in the palace shrines. Ceremonial processions were organized in honour of the gods. A goddess named Potnia (Mistress) was held in particular honour, and in Knossos she appears as the Mistress of the Labyrinth, confirming Evans' belief that the labyrinth of the Minotaur legend was the name of the palace in Knossos. The name appears to be derived from the word *labrys*, which designated the double axe, a ritual object frequently connected with bulls' horns, which was also one of the symbols of the Knossos palace. In Crete the bull, already an object of veneration in Neolithic Çatal-Hüyük in Asia Minor, was transformed from an object of veneration to a sacrificial animal. Games with bulls were very popular, and both young men and women performed dangerous acrobatics in the course of the performance.

An awareness of the power and the glory of Minoan Crete was fertile soil for the flowering of later Greek myths. It was in a Cretan cave that a goat — in another version a nymph — named Amaltheia nursed the baby Zeus, and in gratitude he transformed her horn into the proverbial 'horn of plenty', which was also sometimes depicted as a bull's horn. In the shape of a bull Zeus carried off to Crete the Phoenician princess Europa, and their son Minos was the mythical ruler of Knossos. In order to gain dominion over the whole of Crete, Minos begged Poseidon to send him a bull from the sea, promising to sacrifice the animal to him. When Minos failed to keep his promise, Poseidon avenged the affront by making Pasiphaë, the wife of Minos, fall in love with the bull from the sea. The offspring of this union was the Minotaur, a man with the head of a bull. Minos invited the famous artist Daedalus (*daidalos* means 'artist') to come to Crete from Athens and build him a great retreat for the Minotaur, with many passages — the labyrinth. When the son of Minos was killed in Attica, the ruler of Knossos exacted retribution from the Athenians in the form of seven youths and seven maidens every year, to feed the Minotaur. Theseus, son of the Athenian king, killed the Minotaur and escaped from the Labyrinth with the help of Ariadne, daughter of Minos, who had taken counsel of Daedalus. The wrathful Minos therefore imprisoned Daedalus and his son, Icarus, in the labyrinth, but the ingenious designer made wings for himself and his son, and escaped from Crete to Sicily. Another version has Daedalus and Icarus escaping on small boats which Daedalus equipped with another of his inventions, sails, so that the row-boats sent by Minos could not keep up with the light sailing-craft. Minos nevertheless found Daedalus in Sicily, but lost his life in the process. Greek mythology presents Minos not only as the first ruler to have a large navy at his command, but as the first of all law-givers. After his death he became a judge in the underworld.

In the Middle Bronze Age (Middle Helladic), that is to say roughly during the first four centuries of the second millennium BC, the mainland of Greece seems to have been overshadowed by the Minoan civilization. Ethnically — or perhaps rather, linguistically — it can be assumed that people of Indo-European origin gradually became predominant, the forefathers of the Greeks (Achaeans) who then in the Late Bronze Age extended their domination from Greece itself to Crete as well. At the same time they absorbed much of the material culture as well as religious ideas from the inhabitants settled there before they arrived. There is evidence of trade between Greece and the Cyclades, and Greece and Asia Minor.

In the seventeenth century great changes can be observed in the evolution of the Middle Helladic culture. The small and modestly furnished graves gave way to shaft graves in which the noble dead were surrounded by weapons, cups and jewellery in precious metals, of Minoan origin. This new tendency is seen principally in the shaft graves of the great circle, discovered by Greek archaeologists in 1951–4 outside the citadel walls of Mycenae. Some of these finds, however, transcend the period and belong to the early sixteenth century, to the first phase of the Late Helladic period. Situated on a low hill in the centre of Argolid, half-way between the sites of the Early Neolithic settlements of Lerna and Corinth, Mycenae became the most important centre of Late Helladic culture, and gave its name to the civilization.

The grave furnishings of the shaft graves in the outer ring cannot compare with the magnificent treasures found by Heinrich Schliemann in 1876 in graves inside the Mycenaean citadel (itself dating from a later stage of development, however). These graves date from the sixteenth century, and wealth deposited in them shows how rapidly the power of Mycenae had grown. The remarkable quantities of gold and precious objects of Minoan provenance may have come from looting expeditions by Mycenaean warriors to Knossos, damaged by an earthquake at the beginning of the sixteenth century. We have no reliable proof that these expeditions took place, however.

Some of the finds from the shaft graves of Mycenae show the influence of Egyptian decorative art, and imports from Mycenae have been found in Egypt in strata dating from the sixteenth century BC. Even as the Mycenaean civilization was emerging it must have been in contact with one of the most advanced regions of the Near East. It may have been from Egypt that the use of war chariots in battle strategy, already known in Mesopotamia, came to the Greek mainland. Some scholars even suggest that there were Mycenaean aristocrats fighting in the service of the kings of Egypt of the Eighteenth Dynasty, against the Hyksos.

Further shaft graves have been found in other parts of Greece, in the south-west Peloponnese and on the southern coast of central Greece. The more grandiose circular tombs with a false dome also date from this period, although they become much more frequent in the course of the fifteenth century (in the second phase of the Late Helladic period). Besides those found in Mycenae and several localities in Messenia (south-west Peloponnese), they have been discovered in Laconia (Vaphio) and Thessaly (in the neighbourhood of Iolcus). It was during this period, too, that the Mycenaean aristocrats seized the government of Knossos in Crete.

The Mycenaean civilization reached its highest peak in the fourteenth and thirteenth centuries BC (in archaeological chronology, Late Helladic III A and III B). The centre of cultural advance in the Aegean then shifted to the Greek mainland; palaces were built there, particularly those of Mycenae, Tiryns in the Argolid, Pylos in Messenia (discovered in 1939 on the hill of Ano Englianos) and Thebes in Boeotia. That palaces existed elsewhere as well can be assumed from finds in Iolcus in Thessaly and Orchomenus in Boeotia. Remains of Mycenaean fortifications can be clearly seen on the Acropolis of Athens. Greece was already fairly densely populated by this time; archaeologists have found over five hundred Late Bronze Age settlements on the mainland and the islands. Most of these were agricultural settlements of insignificant size.

In some cases an urban-type settlement was found in the neighbourhood of the palace. An unusual find was that of extensive fortifications surrounding a small palace on Gla hill in Boeotia, in the middle of Lake Kopaïs (now dried up). The fortress seems to have served as a refuge from enemy attack for the people of a considerable area.

The Mycenaean palace was an extensive collection of buildings grouped round the principal building, the residence of the ruler with its courtyard. The characteristic plan of this building was the megaron, of regular ground-plan, with a main hall containing a hearth, and an ante-chamber the entrance to which was usually formed by pillars.

Most of the Mycenaean palaces — Pylos is perhaps the only exception — were fortified with strong walls of large blocks of stone, which later generations of Greeks believed had been set up by giants — Cyclopes. Access to the citadel of Mycenae was through the Lion Gate. The largest known domed tomb has been preserved in Mycenae, the tomb or Treasury of Atreus, over thirteen metres (42½ft) high. The grave furnishings discovered in Mycenaean settlements, unlike Minoan finds, are markedly military in character. The magnificent bronze daggers with gold and silver inlaid ornament were the work of Cretan craftsmen. At the beginning of the 1960s bronze armour was discovered at Dendra in the Argolid, north of Tiryns. From here, too, comes an ornamental gold chalice and other works of art. There were frescoes in the Mycenaean palaces, as in those of Minoan Crete, but in many respects they differed. Besides ritual scenes, the Mycenaean artists portrayed hunting scenes and warlike subjects, complete with war chariots.

Settlements of the Mycenaean type are attested not only in the Cyclades, but on more distant islands like Rhodes, and even in Cyprus. Mycenaean exports of the peak Late Helladic period have been found in Syria, Phoenicia, Palestine, the Jordan valley, Egypt, along the coast of Sicily and southern Italy, and even in Thrace and Macedonia. Finds of Mycenaean pottery in Egyptian tombs dating from the early fourteenth to mid-twelfth century have enabled us to determine the chronology of the output of Mycenaean workshops. It is nevertheless difficult to decide the local provenance of the ware, which retained the same character throughout the area over which the Mycenaean civilization developed.

Records in Linear B script have been found on the Greek mainland as well as in Knossos; a small number come from Tiryns, Orchomenus, Thebes and Eleusis, dozens from Mycenae, and extensive archives were excavated at Pylos in Messenia. At first only inscriptions on potsherds were known from Thebes (as from Tiryns, Orchomenus and Eleusis), but in 1964 tablets were published which appear to date from the fourteenth century BC and are thus the oldest Linear B records in the whole of the Greek mainland. We can judge from this that the palace in Thebes was destroyed earlier than the other Mycenaean centres. Of no less interest are other finds from

Thebes, made in the course of the same excavations: cuneiform cylindrical seals from Babylonia, which prove that the Mycenaean civilization maintained contact with the lands of the Near East.

Linear B tablets found in Pylos have provided invaluable information. They all date from the last year of life of the Pylos palace, and were preserved — as in so many other places — only thanks to the palace burning down. This disaster, the result of enemy attack, happened in about 1200 BC. The area over which the palace at Pylos ruled was roughly that of Messenia later, and supreme power rested with the *vanaka*, i.e. *(v)anax*, ruler, a rank attested from Knossos as well. Some other ranks are also known; a word corresponding to the later Greek *basileus* ('chieftain', 'king') appears on some tablets, although it was a fairly low rank in the hierarchy of Pylos, probably no more than a local manager or bailiff accountable to the palace ruler.

The Pylos records include two terms expressing different types of land ownership. This is probably because there were two distinct forms of land ownership recognized throughout the territory, that of land privately owned, and that owned by the community, designated by the word *damos*, 'people'. The significance of the term for the Mycenaean period is not clear; it would appear that the *damos* embraced the free inhabitants of Pylos, living in the main settlements. A category for the rural population, who were not free, is also given and may have been of pre-Greek origin. Some of the records refer to groups of men, and especially groups of women and children from places far enough away, even from islands in the Aegean or from the coast of Asia Minor. These may have been slaves acquired during military campaigns, but it is not impossible that they were people who had sought refuge in Pylos in the dangerous and uncertain times at the end of the thirteenth century in the Aegean. Whatever explanation we accept, there can be no doubt that the people were completely dependent on the ruler of Pylos, and worked for him. Most of the women and children were housed in Pylos itself, and employed in spinning and weaving. Textiles formed an important part of the economy of the palace.

Pylos, like Knossos, had its flocks of sheep, although on a smaller scale. The principal raw material here was flax, not wool. Other agricultural products were of course important, because the people had to be fed; besides wheat and barley, figs, olives and grapes were cultivated. The tablet records also tell of the crafts and craftsmen, and are thus a commentary to the works of art found by the archaeologists. There are many references to metalworkers, particularly in bronze, and to goldsmiths, potters, cabinet-makers and many other specialized craftsmen.

In Mycenaean Greece, as in Crete, religious practice was bound up with the palace. The Pylos tablets frequently refer to priests and priestesses who perform the rites of the cult, and there is also a special category designated as 'the slaves of the god' (or 'servants of the god'). These individuals were certainly not at the bottom of the social ladder, since they are often referred to as renting private or communally owned land. Religious buildings dating from Mycenaean times have been excavated in Delphi and in one stratum on Delos — that is to say, in localities which later became centres of Greek religious life. In Pylos, as in Knossos, the most venerated figure was the goddess known as Potnia. The Pylos tablets describe her as Mistress (ruler) of the Horses. Tablets from Pylos and from Knossos testify that the Mycenaean Greeks worshipped gods we are familiar with from later Greek history, including Zeus, Hera, Poseidon, Hermes, Artemis, Athena, Dionysus and Ares (Enyalios).

In Mycenaean Greece there does not seem to have been a single state organization; the ruler of each palace governed his own territory. Nevertheless it is quite possible that at least for a time, one of the palace rulers had greater authority than the others. It is likely that the word Achaeans had already been formed in Mycenaean times, to describe the inhabitants of the Greek mainland and islands. This is the most frequently found designation for the Greek warriors in the poems of Homer. In Hittite sources of the second half of the fourteenth and the thirteenth century, there are references to a land called Ahhiyawa; there are various interpretations of these passages, and one frequent hypothesis suggests that Ahhiyawa was on the island of Rhodes. It is worth noting in this connection that even in later times the fortress of Ialysus on Rhodes was known as *Achaia polis*.

Contacts with the Mycenaean civilization are also attested in Troy, in Asia Minor. Troy VI (the sixth layer of occupation identified in the excavations) can best be dated from the end of the nineteenth century and is quite distinct from the culture of the preceding period in the locality. Minyan pottery predominated here in the Middle Bronze Age, and some scholars believe that the people of Troy at this time were of the same ethnic origin as those who brought the Minyan pottery to the Greek mainland. In the second half of the second millennium BC artefacts imported from the Mycenaean sphere appear in Troy. Troy VI was destroyed by an earthquake, probably at the beginning of the thirteenth century; it was soon followed by a new settlement, though a poorer one, known as Troy VIIa. This phase did not last long, dying out after a great fire. It is Troy VIIa that is generally supposed to have been the Troy of Homer; the date assigned to the violent end of this archaeological stratum is uncertain, and varies from the second quarter of the thirteenth to the early twelfth century. The *Iliad* is of course a poetic version of a legend whose historical core is difficult to reconstrue. The view has also been put forward that the real fall of Troy VIIa was not brought about by a military campaign by the Achaeans, but by an attack launched by the 'people of the sea', whose arrival led to far-reaching changes in the Aegean as well as on the mainland of Asia Minor.

Many later Greek myths are connected with the centres of Mycenaean civilization. The story of the Danaids tells of the quarrel between the twin brothers Aegyptus and Danaus, which led Danaus to flee from Egypt to Argos and brought about the murder of the sons of Aegyptus by the daughters of Danaus. Greek mythology attributes the foundation of Mycenae to Perseus the son of Zeus, who performed many great feats. The founder of the line, to which the mythical King Agamemnon, commander of the Achaeans before the walls of Troy, belonged, was Tantalus the son of Zeus, who was said to rule in the western part of Asia Minor. The mythical king of Iolcus in Thessaly was Jason, famous leader of the Argonauts who sailed to far-away Colchis to fetch the Golden Fleece. Thebes was said to have been founded by Cadmus, son of the king of Tyre in Phoenicia, and brother of Europa who belongs to Cretan mythology. Thebes is the scene of the legend of King Oedipus, the man who unknowingly killed his own father and married his own mother; his sons later waged the fratricidal war of Seven against Thebes. The citizens of Thebes successfully defended their city, but it fell to later attackers and was destroyed. According to legend the ruler of Pylos in Messenia was the wise Nestor, oldest of the Achaean leaders in the Trojan War.

CHAPTER II

The End of
the Mycenaean Civilization and
the 'Dark Ages'

Towards the end of the thirteenth century BC the Mycenaean civilization suffered a blow from which it never recovered. Earlier scholars tended to link the end of this civilization with the 'Dorian invasion', that is to say, with the arrival on the Greek mainland of the last wave of Greek-speaking invaders. More recent archaeological research, however, has shown the Dorian settlement of the Peloponnese to be of more recent date; it can thus hardly have anything to do with the catastrophe that befell the Late Helladic centres, upset their economic stability and broke the political power of the Mycenaean rulers.

It was not only the region of the Aegean, however, that was stricken; at about the same period there were signs of decline in other parts of the ancient world. At the end of the thirteenth century the Hittite Empire collapsed, and the lands of Syria and Palestine were hard hit, too. What were the causes behind these far-reaching changes in the eastern Mediterranean?

R. Carpenter recently came forward with an original suggestion. He pointed to the fact that both on the Greek mainland and in Asia Minor people were fleeing from the towns and seeking refuge often very far away. There are references to famine in some of the written sources for this period, and it is Carpenter's hypothesis that the Mycenaean civilization came to an end, as did the Hittite Empire, because of climatic changes which brought drought to Asia Minor, Syria and the Balkan peninsula. Since according to some climatologists similar periods occur at regular intervals of about 1850 years, Carpenter goes on to suggest that later historic changes can also be attributed to the same cause, among them the period of decline after the fall of the Roman Empire and before the upsurge of medieval European civilization.

Although climatic changes certainly played a great part in the way the land was settled, especially in the context of very primitive agriculture, Carpenter's hypothesis is nevertheless too bold, and too little substantiated. Archaeological excavation has shown that the Mycenaean 'forts' on the Peloponnese and in central Greece were refortified in the thirteenth century. Many of them were seriously damaged again before the end of the century, and in some cases there is evidence that this happened twice, on two separate occasions. It is clear that the Mycenaean rulers were afraid of sudden attack, and yet were unable to defend themselves against the final catastrophe. Some scholars believe that the attacks on these centres could have been due to unrest among the rural population, in other words that social upheavals brought the Mycenaean civilization to an end. It has also been suggested that its destruction was due to rivalry and fighting between the rulers of the different Mycenaean centres. This theory is supported by the evidence of tradition as mirrored in the Greek myths, like that of the Seven against Thebes, for example. Not even this explanation can be accepted as quite satisfactory, however.

The most probable explanation remains that which assumes that attack from without destroyed the Mycenaean civilization; recent arguments in favour of this theory have been put forward by V. R. d'A. Desborough, who points out that the Mycenaean rulers took very great precautions against possible enemy attack. It has been proved that during this period water was laid on inside the fortified palaces of Mycenae, Tiryns and Athens, clearly so as to enable the people to withstand a long siege. It would be difficult to keep such measures secret from close neighbours. It would seem more likely that they were dictated by the same fear of enemy attack. One strong argument against the theory of local feuds is the fact that it is in the greatest strongholds that destruction is evident. Of interest in this connection is the discovery of remains of a wall built towards the end of the Late Helladic period, across the Isthmus of Corinth, clearly as a protection against expected attack from the north.

Egyptian sources refer to fighting at the end of the thirteenth century and again in the early years of the twelfth, against invaders who penetrated the Nile delta from the north, from the sea. These 'peoples of the sea' as they are called, seem to have ravaged their way across a large part of Asia Minor, where they laid the Hittite Empire low, and then proceeded through Syria and Palestine to reach Egypt. It is difficult to identify the names of the different groups mentioned by the Egyptian sources. The 'peoples of the sea' seem to have included nomadic tribes of various ethnic origin. The name Puluseta is usually taken to concur with that of the Philistines (Pelishtim), who settled in Palestine at the beginning of the twelfth century, and gave the land its name.

It is at the time when the 'peoples of the sea' were moving along the eastern shores of the Aegean and the Mediterranean that the Mycenaean centres on the Greek mainland were destroyed. Some of the invaders appear to have penetrated into central Greece and the Peloponnese from the north, and dealt the final blow to the Mycenaean civilization. The archaeological material attests a new civilization. It was found, however, that in the last phase of Late Helladic pottery shows signs of the influence of vessels made of organic material, such as are common among nomads. The aim of the invaders seems not to have been territorial conquest, but to get hold of the loot to be found in the forts and palaces of the Mycenaeans. It is not without interest in this connection that the legend of the coming of the Heraclids, the descendants of the great Heracles, at the head of the Dorian invasion of the Peloponnese, speaks of them settling this region at a time three generations after the first invasion, which had been led by the sons of Heracles.

35

Although the invaders probably retreated again, they left such destruction behind them that the inhabitants of the Mycenaean citadels never recovered. If they survived the catastrophe at all, they lived in fear of further attacks for decades. The destruction revealed by excavation of the centres of Mycenaean civilization shows that invasion was repeated. The entire system of Mycenaean power crumbled, and evidence of the material culture shows that the entire way of life changed in Mycenaean Greece, while the population sharply declined. The latest archaeological research enables us to form at least a general idea of the extent of this decline. In the south-west of the Peloponnese, for instance, in Messenia and Triphylia, about 150 settlements are attested during the thirteenth century, while no more than fourteen are known from the twelfth century. The decline in numbers was equally sharp in Boeotia; the number of settlements in Laconia was reduced to a quarter and in the Argolid and the Corinthian region to less than a third. In the middle of the twelfth century the great granary of Mycenae was reduced to ashes, and here as elsewhere the surviving population led a miserable existence among the ruins of their former power and glory.

Besides destruction, decline and general degradation we can also see another tendency. The population began to move from the worst-hit areas to other regions. Settlement became relatively denser, for instance, in mountainous Achaea in the northern Peloponnese, on the island of Cephallenia and probably on the eastern coast of Attica as well. People also migrated in the direction of the Aegean islands, to Chios, Naxos and perhaps to Rhodes as well, and then on to Crete and to Cyprus.

Cyprus was no alien land to the people of Mycenaean Greece, but in earlier times its geographical position naturally brought it within the sphere of eastern influences. This can be seen in the remains of the aceramic Neolithic period found on the southern coast, dating from as early as the sixth millennium BC, and those of other prehistoric cultures which evolved on Cyprus from the middle of the fourth millennium, from Late Neolithic, through Chalcolithic and up to the Bronze Age. The principal influences assimilated came from Asia

Minor and from the territory of Syria and Palestine. The rich deposits of copper were another important factor in the economic and cultural evolution of Cyprus, and undoubtedly contributed to the development of contacts with the Aegean region. As in the latter region, the Bronze Age on Cyprus is divided into three periods. The transition from Early to Middle Bronze Age on Cyprus cannot be reliably determined chronologically as yet; while some scholars date it around the year 2000, others see it as late as the middle of the eighteenth century BC.

Immigrants from Asia Minor were assimilated into the older population, bringing with them a new type of pottery and the knowledge of how to produce and work in bronze. The zoomorphic vessels representing asses, bulls and other animals are particularly interesting. On a clay dish (*pyxis*) from a burial ground in Vounous in northern Cyprus there are the figures of two horses (the front half) with riders. The same necropolis yielded groups of terracotta figures one of which represents ploughing and sowing, and another a sacred place with human figures and sacrificial animals. Copper mining and copper working began in the Early Cypriot period and the metal seems to have been exported to neighbouring areas for the production of bronze from the beginning of the second millennium. Imports from Egypt, Syria and Crete are attested on Cyprus. In the seventeenth century fortifications were built on the island, presumably to defend the people from attack by the Hyksos who were then ruling over Lower Egypt.

The Late Cypriot period began around the year 1600 BC or even as late as the middle of the sixteenth century. In the early years of the fourteenth century, immigrants from the Greek mainland began to settle on Cyprus, and influenced the evolution of the Cypriot civilization considerably. Impulses from Mycenaean culture mingled with those from the east, creating an individual style in pottery; similar tendencies can also be seen in other crafts, particularly carving and jewelry. Alabaster and steatite vessels attained a high level of skill and artistry, as did the richly ornamented bronze tripods and cauldrons. A silver chalice decorated with bulls' heads, lotus blossoms and stylized rosettes was found in the necropolis of one of the largest Late Cypriot settlements at Enkomi, near the eastern coast of the island. The decoration is worked in gold, and the motifs are typical of Mycenaean work. The chalice probably dates from the early fourteenth century BC. An equally beautiful object found in 1962 at Kition in the south-east of the island is the rhyton (a vessel shaped like a bull's horn), dating from about a hundred years later and made of faience decorated in colour with figures of hunters and animals, and stylized flowers.

In the Late Bronze Age period in Cyprus there existed a linear script, the earliest example of which dates from the turn of the sixteenth century. Since it shows certain affinities with the Cretan Linear A, it is known as the Cypro-Minoan script. Several phases of development of the script can be distinguished and it is found at Ugarit in Syria as well as in Crete. Records in this script have survived on pottery shards and on tablets of fired clay, but unlike the Cretan and Mycenaean civilizations, the script on Cyprus does not seem to have been used either for accounts or for trade. The Cypro-Minoan script has not yet been deciphered and so the language — or languages — used in the surviving written records is not known.

After the fall of the Mycenaean civilization groups of Achaeans reached Cyprus. Finds of one of the last types of Late Helladic pottery (III C 1) show that it took the place of the older types produced in Cyprus. Other material remains of Mycenaean origin have also been found, outstanding among them being the royal sceptre of gold and enamel, one of the most wonderful monuments to the skill of the Mycenaean goldsmiths. The architecture of the time also testifies to the growing Achaean influence. In the course of the twelfth century Cyprus seems to have suffered an enemy attack, in the context of the migrations of the 'peoples of the sea', judging from the signs of destruction clearly visible in buildings of the period which have been excavated. Before long, however, new construction began in many places, even if the earlier level was not attained again.

At the beginning of the eleventh century another wave of immigrants from the Aegean reached Cyprus, presumably people from the islands who had been forced to flee before the Dorian expansion. The newcomers were characterized by pottery of the last phase of the Late Helladic period (III C 2), the last expression of the pottery of the dying Mycenaean culture. Cyprus was heavily damaged by an earthquake in the first half of the eleventh century; Enkomi never recovered from the catastrophe, and ceased to exist about the middle of the century. Its place was taken by the newly founded town of Salamis on the coast, not far away, which became one of the most important centres of further development on the island.

There were thus echoes of the heritage of Mycenaean culture for a fairly long time on Cyprus. The arrival of Achaean immigrants strengthened the Greek element and brought the island into the Greek cultural sphere, although influences from the east, especially from Syria and Phoenicia can still be traced. Cyprus was one of the places which maintained a degree of continuity between the Mycenaean and the later Greek traditions. At the same time it was through Cyprus that the people of the Aegean region received cultural impulses from the lands of the Near East. From here, too, knowledge of iron-foundry spread to Crete and Greece, from its beginnings in the Hittite Empire in Asia Minor and Syria.

The situation that now developed in Greece was a complex one. Our present knowledge allows no more than hypotheses. The Achaeans, who had penetrated to the north-west coast of the Peloponnese, moved on to the island of Cephallenia (and perhaps on to Ithaca as well), and were apparently assimilated by the local inhabitants; so the Mycenaean traditions began to weaken. Except for Iolcus in Thessaly and Attica, the Greek mainland was very sporadically settled. There were only small groups scattered over regions which had formerly been well populated, and in some places they were only clinging to an existence in the ruins of their former glory, as was the case in Mycenae.

Economic life broke down in the post-Mycenaean period, and neglected roads fell into disrepair. Nevertheless the tradition of Mycenaean craftsmanship persisted, particularly in pottery. In the second half of the twelfth century what is known as the sub-Mycenaean style emerged; the vessels are much more roughly made, yet the forms and the decoration betray clear signs of the mature Mycenaean pottery tradition. Sub-Mycenaean pottery probably came from the Argolid, and later centred round Athens. The Athenian craftsmen not only drew on the old Mycenaean traditions, but from the first half of the eleventh century were also influenced by pottery from Cyprus.

Finds of material culture show that the people of Athens were deserting the Acropolis to settle in what later became the centre of the city, the Agora, and it is there in the wells and 'culture middens' that much sub-Mycenaean pottery has been found. Another source of evidence of the spread of the type is the necropolis which lay on the site later to become the potters' quarter of Athens, Kerameikos. There are only a few dozen examples of metal objects attested for this period in Athens, but it is interesting that the first ornaments and brooches of iron make their appearance among the bronze pieces. These iron objects, which include a Cypriot sword, supply further evidence of contact between Athens and Cyprus. Apart from this, finds of weapons are very rare for this period.

Unlike most of the rest of the Greek mainland, Athens and its immediate vicinity (Salamis and eastern Attica) were fairly densely settled by the end of the twelfth and the first half of the eleventh century. Groups must have moved in this direction from the Peloponnese, in particular from the Argolid and — if we are to believe the later Greek tradition of the migration of the Neleids, the descendants of Neleus and his son Nestor of Pylos — from Messenia as well.

It appears, however, that the changes which can be observed in the sub-Mycenaean material culture were not only due to decadence of the Mycenaean elements and to influence from the east, but also to the fact that new ethnic groups had appeared on the Greek mainland. Since the Dorians were the most clearly defined of these groups, the phenomenon is usually known as the Dorian migration. In spite of the amount of research devoted to the question, it has not yet proved possible to reconstrue the movements of the Dorians and other related tribes. It can only be assumed that they came from the north of the Balkan peninsula and the alliance of three Dorian tribes later attested in many Dorian communities — the tribes, or *phylae*, of the Hylleis, Dymanes and Pamphyloi — had already been formed before they reached Greece.

This last wave of Greek-speaking immigrants to the mainland brought with it the migration of others towards the islands in the Aegean and the western coast of Asia Minor. In some places the Greek immigrants found earlier settlements dating from Mycenaean times, and on the island of Rhodes and at Miletus we may even assume continuous settlement. Elsewhere elements of Mycenaean culture had persisted in settlements of the local Carian and Lydian peoples who had come into direct contact with the Greeks.

The largest group of Greeks to settle the west coast of Asia Minor were the Ionians. According to Greek tradition they had come there from the northern and western regions of the Peloponnese and from central Greece, particularly from Attica. The two most important Ionian settlements were those of Miletus, where Minoan and Mycenaean pottery has been found, and Ephesus to the north, at the mouth of the river Cayster. Traces of the earliest Greek settlements have not yet been uncovered, although signs of Mycenaean settlement have been found in the vicinity of the temple of Artemis. Colophon, a little further north, also seems to have been settled in Mycenaean times. Although Greek tradition links the first Greek settlement of this area with immigrants from Pylos in the Peloponnese, archaeologists have so far found only pottery of a later phase. Older material has been discovered, however, at Erythrae on the western spur of the peninsula facing the island of Chios. Chios and Samos were also settled by the Ionians. Greek tradition links Chios with immigrants from Euboea and the town of Clazomenae, east of Erythrae, was said to have been founded by people from the Argolid. Phocaea seems to have been settled in a later phase of Ionian migration, and was said to have been founded by people from central Greece and the Peloponnese. These eight settlements, together with four other towns (Myus and Priene on the coast between Miletus and Ephesus, and Lebedus and Teos between Ephesus and Erythrae), formed the Ionian League (*koinon*) in the eighth century BC. It was centred round the Panionion, the temple of Poseidon on the promontory of Mycale, facing the island of Samos.

The Ionians formed the largest and the most important group of Greek communities on the west coast of Asia Minor, and also settled most of the islands in the Aegean. They were related to the inhabitants of the eastern part of central Greece, the island of Euboea and Attica. At the beginning of the sixth century Solon, the Athenian law-giver, still referred to his native town as 'the most ancient land of the Ionians'. The phylae ('tribes') provide important evidence of the fact that the Athenians were related to the Ionians of the islands and of Asia Minor. Up to the end of the sixth century, when Cleisthenes introduced a new system of local phylae, the people of Attica were divided between four tribal phylae, the Geleontes, Hopletes, Argadeis and Aigikoreis. Epigraphic evidence from fifth century Miletus testifies to the existence of two of these phylae there, and quotes a further two phylae, the Oinopes and the Boreis. The Oinopes phyle may have comprised the local people of Asia Minor origin, with whom the Ionians had dealings, while the Boreis phyle is linked in Greek tradition with immigrants from the Peloponnese. All four phylae attested in Attica, as well as the two from Miletus, appear in inscriptions from Cyzicus, a Milesian colony of the first half of the seventh century BC. Other Milesian settlements have also provided epigraphical evidence of the different Ionian phylae.

Further interesting testimony has come from Ephesus, although of a much later date when the city was the capital of the Roman province of Asia. Under the Roman Empire the large population of Ephesus was divided into eight local phylae, one of which bore the name Epheseis and appears to have embraced those who regarded themselves as descendants of the ancient people of the city. This phyle was divided into six *chiliasties* (groups of a thousand) four of which bore the names of Ionian phylae (Argadeis, Geleontes, Boreis and Oinopes). The Geleontes phyle is also attested in Teos and in

Perinthus, a Samian colony founded about the year 600 BC, where the Aigikoreis and Boreis phylae are also found. It is clear that the four basic Ionian phylae already existed at the time of the migration to the western shores of Asia Minor, and the other two must have been formed after the newcomers had settled down in their new home and mingled with the older non-Greek inhabitants of the region.

The calendar also provides evidence of the ancient connection between the people of Attica and the Ionians of Asia Minor and the islands. The different communities in Greece used different names for the months of the year, but some of those from the Athenian calendar also appear in the settlements of the Ionians, in Miletus, Priene, on Samos and some other islands, such as Paros, Delos and Tenos.

The language, too, bears undeniable witness to the relationship ties between the people of Attica and the Ionians of Asia Minor. There were differences between Attic and Ionian in classical times, but linguistic research has shown that they date from after the Ionian migration to the Aegean islands and the shores of Asia Minor. Ionian shows the influence of the languages of the local population in Asia Minor, while certain features of Attic Greek are explained as the result of contact with the Dorian dialect. The Dorian migrations left their mark elsewhere as well. In the western parts of central and northern Greece tribes settled who were related to the Dorians, and traces of Dorian influence are found in Thessaly, and especially in Boeotia. Besides these movements there was migration towards the east in northern Greece. Some of the descendants of the people who settled there in Mycenaean times, and who are usually known as the Aeolians, migrated like the Ionians to the west coast of Asia Minor and the adjacent islands.

One of the oldest Aeolian settlements was that of Smyrna at the mouth of the river Hermus. Later it was conquered by the people of Colophon and came into the Ionian sphere of influence. It did not become a member of the Ionian League, however. Smyrna was overrun by King Alyattes of Lydia at the beginning of the sixth century BC, and from then onwards remained a mere village. It was not until the Hellenistic age that the new Smyrna was built a few kilometres south of the old one. The most important centre of Aeolian settlement in Asia Minor was the island of Lesbos, where a few settlements may have existed even before the arrival of the Greeks, the most important being that of Mytilene. The oldest Aeolian settlement on the mainland seems to have been Cyme. Like the Ionians, the Aeolians kept close links with the local population and later formed the Aeolian League.

While the north-west tribes settled the western regions of northern and central Greece, the Dorians settled most of the Peloponnese, particularly the southern and eastern parts. They did not remain only on the mainland, however, but migrated to the southern islands of the Aegean, particularly to Crete, Melos, Thera, Cos and Rhodes, and also dominated the south-west coast of Asia Minor, where their most important settlement was that of Halicarnassus.

Thus at the turn of the second millennium BC, along with the changes that followed the decline of the Mycenaean civilization, and as a result of the Dorian migrations and the movement of population towards the islands in the Aegean and the west coast of Asia Minor, a picture of settlement in Greece emerges which is to remain constant for a long time to come. An important source of information on the mutual relationships between the different tribal groups comes from the study of Greek dialects. In spite of the lack of reliable data in some cases, and doubts about how to interpret some linguistic phenomena, research can put forward probable conclusions about the groups of tribes and their respective groups of dialects.

Descendants of the Mycenaean Achaeans, whose language is recorded on tablets inscribed with Linear B, lived on in the mountains of Arcadia in the inner Peloponnese and on the island of Cyprus. Linguistic analysis of their written records suggests that Arcadian and Cypriot were a direct continuation of the language spoken by the people of Mycenaean Greece. Closely related to them were the Ionians, who lived in Attica and Euboea and later moved to settle a broad band of islands in the Aegean and much of the west coast of Asia Minor. The third group comprised the Aeolians, descendants of the people who lived in northern Greece in Mycenaean times; they are found in Thessaly, Boeotia, and later on the island of Lesbos and the adjacent parts of the coast of Asia Minor. In Thessaly and Boeotia, however, they were intermixed to a considerable degree with the last wave of Greek immigration, representing the fourth linguistic group. The northern branch was formed by the north-west tribes, who settled in Phocis, Locris, Aetolia and Acarnania in central Greece, and later on neighbouring islands in the Ionian Sea. In Epirus they were very mixed with the local Illyrian population. In the Peloponnese Achaea in the north and Elis in the north-west formed the linguistic bridge between the north-west tribes and the Dorians. Elsewhere in the peninsula, except for Arcadia, the Dorians were predominant, even if in some places they had to come to terms with the earlier Achaean settlers.

The Dorian migration must be seen as the gradual penetration of Greece by the Dorians and their relatives, the north-west tribes. There are no finds of material culture that can be reliably linked to this final wave of Greek immigration, but this is no argument to prove it did not take place. It is always difficult to link a specific type of archaeological find with a certain ethnic group, especially in a period which has left no written records. It must also be borne in mind that the Dorians and the other related tribes were nomads who left little trace of their material culture. It can be assumed that they invaded the Greek mainland during the sub-Mycenaean period, that is to say from the late twelfth century up to the second half of the eleventh.

While up to the end of this period sub-Mycenaean vessels are the most frequent finds in excavated settlements and burial grounds, in the second half of the eleventh century a new style emerges, known as Protogeometric pottery. The makers of this Protogeometric ware seem to have been Attic potters. The Protogeometric amphorae are of similar form to those of the sub-Mycenaean culture, but more slender and more carefully finished. A faster potter's wheel was needed to make them, brushes were used to execute the ornament, as had already been done on Cyprus, and compasses were used to trace the design. The combination of these two techniques created a revolution in pottery decoration. Protogeometric pottery, which was perfected in the course of the tenth century, was the first step along the road to the magnificent Geometric style of the early archaic period. Throughout this time Attica retained its leading position in pottery.

The Protogeometric style also marks the beginning of the Iron Age in Greece. At the end of the eleventh century BC the crafts began to revive after a decline of almost two hundred years, and tendencies emerged which led to a new upsurge of material culture. Protogeometric pottery has been found even in the oldest strata of some of the settlements founded by Ionian and Aeolian immigrants on the western shores of Asia Minor and on the adjacent islands in the Aegean Sea.

In spite of the decline which set in after the fall of the Mycenaean centres, and in spite of abrupt changes in the character and density of settlement due to the sharp fall in the population of mainland Greece followed by the immigration of new tribes, it is possible to trace a measure of continuity — even if faint at times — between the civilization of the Mycenaean Achaeans and Greek civilization proper, which began to evolve at the turn of the second millennium. Besides pottery, ship-building is also proof of this progress. The isolated pictures of boats in the decoration of Protogeometric and Geometric pottery show the same basic features as those adorning Mycenaean and sub-Mycenaean pottery. There can be no doubt that the migrations of the Mycenaean Achaeans in the twelfth century, as well as later contacts between the Greek mainland and Cyprus, and finally the founding of Aeolian, Ionian and later also Dorian settlements on the coast of Asia Minor, could not have taken place without knowledge of ship-building. The Greeks continued the expansionist contacts of the Mycenaean sailors, and the Aegean became more than a sea-route; it became a lively and integral part of the Greek world.

At the beginning of the ninth century BC the Geometric style began to appear in Attica, the Argolid, the islands of the Aegean and the west coast of Asia Minor. The shapes and the decoration of the vessels developed naturally from those of the Protogeometric style, but at the same time entirely new elements with no trace of the sub-Mycenaean heritage can be seen. The Geometric style gradually spread to other localities as well (Corinth, Boeotia, Thessaly); techniques were perfected, the number of types of vessels increased, and the ornament developed in great variety, with realistic elements added to Geometric motifs. The Geometric period is usually divided into three or four phases, the culminating phase lasting into the eighth century BC, the beginning of the archaic period.

Metal-working also made great progress, as can be seen from finds of iron swords and spearheads. From the middle of the ninth century conical bronze helmets take the place of leather headgear, and bronze was used for vessels, especially for goblets and cooking-pots. The jewelry found in a woman's grave in the Agora, in Athens, probably dating from mid-ninth century, shows the high degree of skill reached by the goldsmiths, while excavation has revealed the level attained by architecture, too; Old Smyrna is of particular interest, having been an urban settlement with walled defences as early as the ninth century BC.

Towards the end of the ninth century the Greeks began to make contact with the Near East. Cyprus played an important role as an intermediary, with its established relations with Crete, the Aegean region, and metropolitan Greece on the one hand, and with Syria and Phoenicia on the other. Archaeological excavation of Al-Mina at the mouth of the Orontes has yielded interesting testimony to Greek penetration of the eastern coast of the Mediterranean. The town has been identified with Poseideion, which Herodotus (3,91) situated 'on the border between Cilicia and Syria'. Al-Mina was founded about the middle of the ninth century, and it is from this period that the finds of material culture date, pointing to links with Phoenicia, northern Palestine and Cyprus. Greek Geometric pottery seems to have appeared in Al-Mina from the end of the ninth century. The Greeks thus came into direct contact with the people of Syria and the neighbouring regions. In the eighth century Al-Mina came within the sphere of influence of the powerful kingdom of Urartu, the centre of which lay on the Armenian plateau. Urartu possessed rich metal deposits, and metal-working reached a high level, as can be seen from the works of art in bronze decorated with gold leaf.

A new and unknown world was opened to the Greeks when they reached the shores of Syria, and like the Minoan Cretans and the Mycenaean Achaeans before them, they assimilated elements of the rich cultural traditions of the Near East. The long 'Dark Ages' had finally come to an end, and a great upsurge of creative activity began among the people of the Greek communities. This new phase of Greek civilization is reflected not only in the monuments of material culture, but in the fact that the Greeks acquired an alphabet.

Linear B, the earliest known record of the Greek language, fell into oblivion with the destruction of the Mycenaean centres and their palace economies. The script that now evolved in Greece was much simpler, and at the same time much more sophisticated, than the clumsy syllabic script which often only partly expressed the sounds of the Greek, and was used almost exclusively for economic and administrative texts. It was an alphabet which was relatively easy to learn and which was well suited to the needs of the Greek language.

Greek tradition kept alive the idea that the Greeks had taken over their alphabet from their eastern neighbours. Herodotus (5, 58f) says that the Greeks learned to write from the Phoenicians who invaded Boeotia with Cadmus, who founded the city of Thebes. As often happens in Greek myths, the ancient Mycenaean tradition — which has been partially confirmed by archaeological evidence — has become mixed up with the later records of Greek contacts with the eastern Mediterranean. According to Herodotus the Greeks called the script they adopted 'Phoenician' letters.

Until recently the view that the Greek alphabet was of Phoenician origin was considered well-founded, but closer study of the Semitic alphabet and its relation to the Greek alphabet, based on newly found evidence, suggests that the genesis of the Greek alphabet was not quite so simple. The Greeks appear to have drawn principally on the Aramaic alphabet of North Syria, which in addition to signs for the consonants sometimes also used signs for the vowels, a feature of

48

Early Neolithic marble figurine from Attica. Height 22.5cm (8¾in).
Archaeological Museum, Eleusis.

Cycladic marble statuette of a harp-player
from Keros, about 2500 BC. Height 22.5cm (8¾in).
National Museum, Athens.

50

Krater, or large wine bowl,
in the Kamares style, but with unusual sculpted flowers,
from Phaestus, about 1800 BC. Height 45.5cm (18in).
Archaeological Museum, Heraklion.

Opposite above
Gold cup from Vaphio, Laconia, of Cretan workmanship,
showing the trapping of a wild bull, 1500–1400 BC. Diameter 10.8cm (4¼in).
National Museum, Athens.
Opposite below
Ivory figure of an acrobat springing over a bull, from Knossos,
about 1600–1500 BC. Length 24.5cm (9¾in).
Archaeological Museum, Heraklion.
Above left
Fresco of a fisherman, from Thera, about 1500 BC.
Height of figure 107.5cm (3ft 6¼in).
National Museum, Athens.
Above right
Bronze statuette of a praying youth, from Tylissus,
Crete, about 1500 BC. Height 15.2cm (6in).
Archaeological Museum, Heraklion.

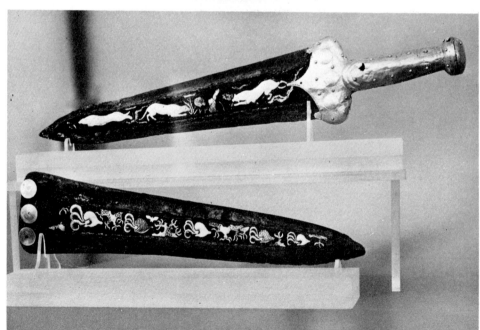

Above
Silver cup from Enkomi inlaid in gold and niello, about 1400 BC.
Diameter 15.7cm (6in). Cyprus Museum, Nicosia.
Above left
Gold seal ring from Mycenae, showing seated goddess and worshippers,
1500–1400 BC. Width 3.4cm (1¼in). National Museum, Athens.
Below left
Two daggers from near Pylos, one with gold hilt intact and showing
leopards hunting, the other with the blade only, depicting nautiluses
among rocks, about 1500 BC. Length of top dagger 32cm (12½in).
National Museum, Athens.

Geometric krater from Athens
showing a funeral procession, about 750 BC. Height 123cm (4ft ½in).
National Museum, Athens.

great importance for the formation of the Greek alphabet. Recently scholars have also pointed out affinities between early forms of the Greek alphabet and what is known as the Early Canaanite alphabet (from Palestine), which seems to have been the source of the Semitic alphabets.

The earliest known documents of Greek texts written in the alphabet date from the second half of the eighth century BC and so it can be assumed that this alphabet was formed about the middle of the century, or probably somewhat earlier. The older and simpler idea that the Greeks had received this new type of script directly from the Phoenician merchants who traded in the Aegean has now given way to the assumption that a longer period of contact with Semites was needed before the alphabet could be evolved. Some scholars interpret the finds of Semitic imports of the ninth and eighth centuries on Crete and Rhodes as indicating the existence of Semitic settlements there at that time. A more probable theory, however, is that which assumes the Syrian coast, and in particular Al-Mina, as the locality in which the Greeks came to know the Semitic Aramaic alphabet. It was not until a later stage in the evolution of the Greek alphabet that the Phoenician letters influenced it; the signs for the diphthongs ks, ps, kh, ph (the letters ξ, ψ, χ, φ) are closest to the Phoenician, and the names for the letters of the Greek alphabet have also been taken from Phoenician. The forms of different but related Semitic systems are also probably reflected in some of the differences occurring between early alphabets from different regions of the Greek world.

The alphabet was not used merely for day-to-day trade, but very soon served a literary purpose as well. It is characteristic that the earliest evidence of the use of the alphabet comes from comic rhymed inscriptions on vases. Both the hexameter on a Geometric pitcher from Athens, and the incompletely preserved lines of verse on a Geometric goblet from one of the first Greek colonies on the island of Pithecusae (now Ischia) off the south-west coast of Italy, were written in the twenties of the eighth century.

This is most probably the period during which the Homeric epic poems were composed. In antiquity there were already arguments about where and when Homer was born, and there were even doubts as to whether he had ever really lived. In modern times scholars have put forward many theories to account for the Homeric poems, from those who stress the inconsistencies and conflicting features in the description of what happened before Troy and on Ithaca and conclude that the epic is a collection of shorter separate poems, to those who attribute the *Iliad* and the *Odyssey* to Homer alone. In between these two extremes a wide range of theories have been put forward to explain how the poems came into existence.

Archaeology, starting from the amazing discoveries of Heinrich Schliemann in Troy and Mycenae, has provided much valuable information about the material culture at the end of the Mycenaean period, the time in which the poems are set, and in the centuries which followed. It is now possible to compare with actual historical remains the descriptions of buildings, things of daily use, artistic objects, and weapons, given in the Homeric epics. Literary scholarship has also developed, making use of analyses of such mediaeval epics as the Song of Roland, the Song of the Nibelungs, and the chivalrous epics of Yugoslavia. Linguistic aspects and questions of style have also been thoroughly studied.

When Linear B was deciphered it opened a new chapter in the history of Homeric studies. Here was proof that the Mycenaean civilization was the creation of Greek-speaking people, and evidence of ancient traditions in Greek culture, especially some religious ideas. At the same time it became clear that Mycenaean society, as far as we can reconstruct it from the fragmentary evidence of clay tablets found in the ruins of the palaces, was very different from that depicted in the *Iliad* and the *Odyssey*. Opinion is still sharply divided on the question of the origin of the epic poems, and particularly on that of how far they can be used to form a picture of the historical reality of early Greek civilization. Some scholars stress those passages which can be related to the finds of material Mycenaean culture, thus pointing to the antique character of much of Homer's detail. Others consider those details to be more significant, which can be related to later archaeological evidence, and find more parallels between the world of

Homer and the Geometric period, the time when Greek civilization was reviving again.

Even if we cannot say with certainty who Homer was and what part he played in the composition of the epics attributed to him, we can say that they came into being – that is to say, in the form in which they have come down to us – in the middle or the second half of the eighth century. It is usually thought that the *Iliad* is one or even two generations earlier than the *Odyssey*, which does not mean that they could not have been composed by the same poet. The epics may have been written down at that time, or a little later, although some alterations were certainly made as time went on, principally by those who recited the poems. From the middle of the sixth century BC the poems were recited at the Great Panathenaea in Athens. The text was studied and edited again carefully in Alexandria, in Hellenistic times.

The perfection of the hexameter form, the wealth of imagery and means of expression, and the dramatic liveliness of the narration testify to mature and masterly craftsmanship such as only a long tradition of the epic could produce. The *Iliad* and the *Odyssey* stand at the summit of the evolution of oral poetry. It is likely that bards were already composing heroic epics to the accompaniment of the lyre in Mycenaean times. It is not without interest in this respect, that one of the frescoes discovered in Pylos shows a man with a lyre; it may be the figure of a god. A few of the formulae (repeated phrases), describing objects not found in later periods, are also probably of Mycenaean origin, like *fasganon argyroelon*, 'a sword decorated with silver studs'.

The art of epic poetry was not entirely lost later, and persisted in environments where certain Mycenaean traditions survived. When settlement of the coast of Asia Minor brought the Ionian and Aeolian population into direct contact with lands which had formerly been in the Mycenaean sphere, these traditions were strengthened still further, and continued to develop. These contacts — and conflicts — were the source of new experience which found its way into the old story. It was in this environment that the legends connected with Troy were born. As one of the foremost literary historians, Albin

Lesky, has aptly remarked, 'a saga postulates ruins'. The fact that epic poetry evolved in an Asia Minor environment can be seen, too, from the language of Homer, where Ionian features are more prevalent than Aeolisms and Achaeisms. Indeed, the tradition of antiquity had it that Homer came from the western shores of Asia Minor. The well-known distich (couplet) tells us how seven cities fought for the honour of being Homer's birthplace, and classical sources give us the names of twenty cities which claimed this distinction. The biographies are unanimous, however, in placing the great poet in the area where the Ionian and the Aeolian elements met, and specifically in Smyrna and Chios, where the Homeridae, the professional declaimers of his verse, are attested.

In the *Iliad* and the *Odyssey* the poet has tried to describe as faithfully as possible the lost Mycenaean civilization. The epic tradition kept alive knowledge of the existence of great cities in Mycenae, Pylos, and other places of the world as it was then known. Individual works of art and weapons or armour are described, which were Mycenaean. Either these are reminiscences which persisted in the epics, or perhaps there were rare examples of ancient objects which survived into a later period. Very often, however, the desire for realism remained superficial; implements and weapons are said to be of bronze, because bronze was known to be the material most used in Mycenaean times. At the same time we read of articles made of iron, and the poems refer to the technique of iron-working, which the Greeks did not know until the end of the second millennium BC. There are similar anachronisms in the descriptions of the fighting before the walls of Troy. Homer's heroes ride to battle in their chariots, yet they do not use them in battle, as was common in Mycenaean times, but meet their enemies in combat on foot.

Odysseus has slaves in his house, and especially slave girls; his wealth is principally in his flocks and herds. But there is no trace of the Mycenaean palace bureaucracy, and the figures given are far lower than those we find on tablets from Pylos and Knossos. The reality of Mycenae has been lost in the experience of later ages and ideas, and transformed into the heroic age of myth. Society as described by the two epic poems is thus the reflection of a long epic tradition and, as such, a figment of the poet's imagination. It is not easy to distinguish the elements which go to make up this artificial construction. In general it can be said that the principal features are those which were characteristic for the time in which the legends of Troy took on epic form in the Ionian and Aeolian milieu.

The society Homer depicts was decidedly aristocratic. Each tribal group, settled in a definite area, was headed by the *basileus*; he held in his hands the administrative, military and priestly power, and had the final word in the council (*boule*), whose members seem to have been the elders of smaller groups with kinship ties. The people's assembly (*agora*) had no powers, and in peacetime as in wartime the common people played a passive role. The basic economic unit was the royal household (*oikos*), which was self-supporting to a degree, and patriarchal in character. The common people were engaged mainly in agriculture and tending their flocks. The craftsmen, too, worked for the basileus and his household. At the bottom of the social ladder were the nomadic labourers (*thetes*) and the slaves. There was little trade, and that was in the hands of Phoenician merchants. The basileis did not trade, but exchanged gifts as an expression of their mutual admiration and friendly hospitality.

Homeric poems put the whole of the Greek world before us, in all its breadth and variety, bathed in the light of poetry. Heroes appear there, but they are men of flesh and blood, with all the good and bad qualities of human beings. The gods appear too, often taking upon themselves the friendliest forms in their contacts with human beings. The world of the gods is a major element in Homer's Greece. Everything they do is an organic part of the story and, in both poems, understandable from the human point of view. It is one of the characteristic features of Homer's epics that man is closely bound up with nature and with life, with labour and with battle, with relaxation and with fun.

The *Iliad* and the *Odyssey* are of outstanding importance for Greek culture. They mark the end of the long period of oral epic tradition. The *aoidoi* (bards) improvising to the accompaniment of the lyre are

61

replaced by the *rhapsodes* (reciters) whose text is predetermined. The Homeric poems became the common property of the Greek nation. The young people learned their heroic past from the epics, which provided poets and artists with their source of inspiration. The heroic age as Homer described it in the *Iliad* and the *Odyssey* became the prime source of classical mythology. As long as classical Greek civilization endured, Homer was the most famous and most widely read author. This was especially so for the *Iliad*, the text most frequently found copied on Egyptian papyri.

The peak phase of the Geometric style, the penetration of Greek merchants to the eastern Mediterranean, the evolution of the Greek alphabet and, not least, the great epic poems, are all expressions of the approach of a new era, an era which came into its own in the archaic age. The rise of the city-states (*poleis*) was the expression of a fundamental tendency of the time; nevertheless the different regions of Greece developed their own distinctive characteristics.

CHAPTER III

Sparta and Dorian Crete

In the present state of our knowledge we cannot reliably say how the Dorian tribes arrived in the Peloponnese. Some scholars thought the Dorians came from Crete to settle in southern Greece, but today it is widely accepted that it was from central Greece that they arrived in the Peloponnese, and that one of the first regions they occupied was the Argolid. From here their influence seems to have spread both to the north, the isthmus of Corinth, and southwards into Laconia. Their incursions brought them into touch with whatever remnants of the old Achaean population were still to be found in the Peloponnese.

In Mycenaean times life in Laconia had naturally centred on the valley of the Eurotas. The palace of Therapne, standing on a hill not far from the left bank of the middle reaches of this river, fell to unknown assailants who were probably the men who overthrew Mycenae, Tiryns and Pylos about this time. It was not until the end of the eighth century BC that attention was again drawn to the region, for it was then that the Dorian Spartans took up the ancient traditions of Laconia. Therapne then saw the emergence of a cult of Menelaus, the mythical ruler of Lacedaemon whose wife, Helen, was the legendary incentive behind the Achaeans' assault upon the walls of Troy. There were, however, places in Laconia where settlement had been continuous, and foremost among these was Amyclae, on the right bank of the Eurotas, south of the Mycenaean centre at Therapne.

The Dorians arrived in Laconia in the tenth century BC and settled about 8 kilometres (5 miles) north of Achaean Amyclae, on a spot which can be seen from the hill where the proud residence of the Mycenaean rulers of Laconia once stood. This was the cradle of Dorian Sparta, also known as Lacedaemon. A certain quantity of shards of Mycenaean pottery have been found there, but it cannot be said with any certainty that the place was already permanently settled at this time. The earliest Dorian settlement, on the other hand, is reliably attested by finds of Protogeometric pottery.

Most probably the new rulers of Laconia were shepherds, and their move from the Argolid was in search of suitable land to settle. When they became masters of the fertile Eurotas valley they subjugated the Achaean peasants they found settled there. We do not know exactly how this happened, but we can assume that this invasion by a group of Dorian tribes laid the foundations for the social system which developed in Sparta, and that the enslaved rural population became the *helots*.

The Dorian conquerors seem to have behaved the same way in other places, too, for a similar relationship is found elsewhere, and particularly on Crete. Even from Dorian cities whose social structure differed considerably from that of Sparta later there is evidence that the Dorian invaders enslaved some of the earlier Achaean settlers.

In Argos, for instance, one of the earliest Dorian cities in the Peloponnese, there were *gymnetes*, or *gymnesioi*, who were compared to the helots of Sparta by the later writers Julius Pollux (late second century AD) and Stephanus of Byzantium (sixth century AD). It is usually assumed that Herodotus was referring to them when he told (6, 83) of 'everything being in the hands of slaves' for a time in Argos, at the beginning of the fifth century. A similar section of the population is attested in Sicyon, which according to tradition had been invaded by Dorians from Argos. Pollux and Stephanus called

these people *korynephoroi*, while elsewhere Pollux, like the historian
Theopompus (fourth century BC), uses the term *katonakophoroi*. The
former term (*koryne* means a 'club' or 'stick'), like the word *gymnetes*
(meaning 'naked' or 'barely clad'), shows that in Argos and in Sicyon
these men were at the bottom of the social ladder, and probably
served as light-armed infantry. The second term from Sicyon comes
from the word *katonake*, the coarse woollen garment worn by
country people. Perhaps the derisive appellation *konipodes* (meaning
'dusty feet') belongs to the same category; it was used by the people
of Dorian Epidaurus in the eastern part of the Argolid, to describe the
country people of the vicinity.

We know nothing more about these social groups. It is possible
that the comparison with the helots made by later sources is a superficial one. Some scholars believe that unlike the helots, the peasants of
Sicyon, Argos and Epidaurus enjoyed personal freedom and were not
bound to the land. It is hardly possible to doubt that they were the
descendants of the earlier settlers, the Achaeans, and that they lived in
subjection to the Dorian invaders.

There is also interesting evidence from some of the colonies
founded by Dorian cities. In the list of groups of subjugated peoples
given by Pollux and some other writers, we find the name of the
Mariandynoi, who lived on the north-west coast of Asia Minor and
were overrun by the people of Heracleia Pontica, a settlement
founded in the sixth century by men from the Dorian city of Megara,
between Corinth and Attica. The Mariandynoi are described as
dorophoroi ('bearing gifts') because they delivered a specified quota to
their masters. The Bithynians of Asia Minor were also said to have a
similar status to that of the helots; they had been subjugated by other
Megarian colonists, the citizens of Byzantium, the most important
fortified place on the Bosphorus, founded as early as the seventh
century BC. Finally the Kyllyrioi, or Killikyrioi, are noteworthy in
this connection; they were the original settlers in the region of
Syracuse, founded in the second half of the eighth century by Dorian
Corinth. According to Herodotus the Kyllyrioi were the slaves of the
gamoroi, the landowners of Syracuse.

65

The Dorians were not alone in this respect. The other related tribes, who penetrated the northern and central regions of Greece at the end of the second millennium BC, also took over not only the land they overran but the established population as well. The *penestai*, who worked the land owned by their Thessalian masters, are most often compared to the helots of Sparta. The *woikiatai* of Locris seem to have lived under similar conditions, and so perhaps did the Kylikranes who lived in Trachis, near the Malian Gulf.

Although our information about the status of these different groups of servile peoples is very fragmentary, it is clear that the Spartan helots were not an isolated phenomenon. Nor is it mere coincidence that subjugated peasants, without full rights, are attested mainly in regions settled by the Dorians or tribes related to them, from the north-west. This should not be taken to mean that this form of servile status had anything to do with particular features of the Dorian invaders, still less any 'racial' superiority on their part. It is sufficient to recall that in the seventh and sixth centuries BC Sicyon, Corinth and Megara were troubled by similar social problems to those faced at the same period by Ionian Miletus or Aeolian Mytilene, and that these problems were dealt with more or less in the same way. The answer to the question why a servile peasant population was formed mainly in Dorian cities must be sought in the general situation obtaining in Greece at the turn of the second millennium BC, and particularly in the stage of development of the Dorian and related tribes at that time.

We have already seen that the Dorians were probably shepherds at the time they arrived in Greece. When they conquered arable land in the valley of the Eurotas they divided it up between them, in such a way as to give each man the same share. The land won by the Dorians in the course of their invasion of Laconia was known as 'civic land' (*politike chora*), and the individual lots (*klaroi*) were distributed among the citizens of Sparta for cultivation. Although these holdings became hereditary in later times, the tradition persisted that the land did not belong to the individual citizen but to the phyle, or rather, to the group of all three Dorian phylae. In Plutarch's *Life of Lycurgus*

(16) we read that the father could not decide the fate of the child born to him, but was obliged to bring the babe to where the elders of the phyle were gathered. The elders not only examined the child to decide whether it was strong and healthy enough to be allowed to live, but at the same time allotted the boy his share of the land. A first-born son was probably given the family *klaros*, but there were other possible solutions. We know from Polybius (12, 6b, 8) that there was an old Spartan custom by which several brothers shared the same wife. In itself polyandry is one of the many ancient survivals in the Spartan social system, but it is also related to the question of land tenure. In the legal code of the Cretan city of Gortyn, reminiscent in many points of Spartan society, there is direct evidence that several brothers could manage the family land together.

Classical writers regarded the material equality of all citizens as a fundamental feature of the Spartan regime, linking it either directly to the invasion of Laconia by the Dorians, or attributing it to the mythical ruler Lycurgus, believed to have created that regime. At the same time they were aware that there were exceptions to the rule. In his account of the Lacedaemonian constitution Xenophon (15, 3) said that the Spartan kings 'set aside land in many perioecic (surrounding) towns'. Scholars are not agreed on the meaning of this remark. It is well known, however, that when the Spartans penetrated further into the peripheral regions of Laconia, they no longer added to the 'civic land'. They also left the local population as free men. At the same time there seem to have been estates there which became the private property of the Spartan kings and perhaps of some of the nobles as well.

The principal agricultural land was the 'civic land' in the Eurotas valley; the Spartans lived on the produce of their holdings, cultivated by the helots. Like the land, the helots were also the property of the tribes of the Dorian conquerors. Pausanias (3, 20, 6) called them the 'slaves of the whole body' of Lacedaemonians; for Strabo (8, 365) they were 'some kind of state slaves', while Pollux (3, 83) placed the helots, *penestai* and similar groups of subjugated peasants somewhere 'between the freemen and the slaves'. The same hesitation can be seen in the modern literature. The helots are most frequently described as state slaves or serfs, yet neither category entirely fits the case. Unlike the state slaves, who were exclusively in the power of the *polis* which owned them, the helots were allotted to individual Spartan citizens along with their share of the land. The tenant of the klaros was thus automatically the master of his helots. The main difference between the helots and the serfs of mediaeval feudalism was that the former were not part of the nation, but were natives enslaved by foreign invaders and robbed of their freedom in the same way as slaves. Helotry was thus a specific form of subjection which emerged when agricultural land and the peasants who cultivated it were conquered by invaders who were not yet a settled people and had not yet fully developed the idea of private property.

The helots were obliged to deliver their quota to the Spartans in kind. From the figures given by Plutarch in his *Life of Lycurgus* (8), the tenant of a holding received 70 *medimni* of barley annually, and his wife received 12 medimni; in addition the helots sent the master an unspecified amount of 'liquid produce', presumably milk and wine, and perhaps cheese and figs. It is thought that the quotas were fixed in Aeginetan medimni, which would mean that every married Spartan received about 100 cwt of barley as well as a considerable quantity of other agricultural produce. On the basis of this account and some other comments in classical authors many writers have tried to work out the average size of an allotment of land, the number of such grants, and thus to arrive at an estimate of the density of settlement in Sparta. It is safe to say that particularly after they had conquered Messenia the Spartans had several thousand klaroi, while the numbers of the helots must have been several times greater than the number of the Spartan citizens.

Helotry was often criticized by classical authors. Plutarch described the treatment of the helots as 'the cruellest and most illegal system'. The Spartans were said to force the helots to drink too much wine and then hold them up as an awful example to young Spartans. In the same way they forced them to sing immoral songs and dance ridiculous dances. The helots were made to wear special garments and were whipped annually to remind them that they were slaves. The relations between helot and Spartan were most succinctly described by the saying that in Sparta the free were the freest and the slaves (i.e. the helots) the most enslaved.

The *ephors*, the highest officials in Sparta, declared war on the helots every year at the beginning of their year of office, in order to legalize the killing of helots. This measure is in itself proof that the Spartans were aware of having conquered the helots by military invasion. The declaration of war was accompanied by a series of disciplinary measures against the helots known as the *krypteia* (from *krypteuein*, 'to hide'). The most resourceful young Spartans were sent out into the countryside with no more than a dagger and the minimum of food. During the daytime they scattered and rested in hiding, to emerge on the roads at night and kill any helots who came their way. They would move through the countryside, often killing the strongest and toughest men.

Aristotle associated the krypteia with Lycurgus, but Plutarch seems to have been unwilling to attribute this cruel institution to his hero, and suggested that it was a consequence of the great helot rebellion of the sixties of the fifth century BC. The real origin of the krypteia seems to be very ancient, however. Certain scholars have shown that the initiation rites of primitive peoples in many continents have similar features. Among Malayan tribes, for example, the youth who wanted to ensure his entry into the society of adult men had to kill a slave girl.

Like other survivals from tribal days the krypteia served a new function in Sparta, becoming part of the military training which was directed at the preservation of the existing order. Probably the punitive campaigns took place at times when the helots were thought to be a particular danger. As Thucydides said in his account of the War of the Peloponnese (4, 80), the Spartans were constantly worried about their internal security, mainly because of the helots. According to some reports, the Spartans never laid aside their arms, and were constantly on the alert to prevent them falling into the hands of the helots. The doors of their houses were furnished with bolts to help them resist unexpected attack. Little wonder, then, that the helots (in the words of the historian Theopompus) were 'wild and hostile in their manner' towards the Spartans. And in his account of the unsuccessful rising plotted at the beginning of the fourth century by the impoverished Spartan Cinadon, Xenophon remarked that the hatred of the helots and other oppressed and subordinated groups for the Spartans was so fierce that 'they would have liked to eat them, even raw'.

All these comments aptly convey the social tensions and class antagonisms rife in Sparta particularly during the classical period. It should be mentioned, on the other hand, that there were helots working in their masters' households, and examples can be found of a good relationship between them. Helots also served as light infantry and as rowers in the Lacedaemonian fleet. There were many helots fighting side by side with the Spartans against the Persians, for example, in the victorious battle of Plataea in 479 BC. During the Peloponnesian War, however, many helots deserted to the Athenian side, to which the Spartans reacted in two ways: some were sent to fight in other sectors, and were then freed from their servitude and given further military duties, but large numbers of these helots who had deserved their freedom were secretly put to death.

There were also perioeci (*perioikoi*) in the Spartan army, who like the Spartans were called Lacedaemonians; the term means 'those who live round about', and they inhabited the mountainous regions bordering the Eurotas valley, and the coastal area. When the Spartans conquered Messenia they made the people of the peripheral regions into perioeci, too. There were several dozen perioecic cities, with their autonomous administration. Although the perioeci were free men, they took no part in the administration of the Spartan state. There is no reliable evidence as to their ethnic origins; some scholars believe them to have been the descendants of the Achaeans settled in the surrounding parts of the country, while others see Dorians in them, as in the Spartans. Probably neither view corresponds to the reality; remnants of the Achaeans seem to have survived among the perioeci, particularly in southern Laconia, but the Dorian element

70

was certainly very strong. The perioecic cities varied both in size and in their ethnic composition.

Like the people of other Greek cities, the perioeci were primarily agricultural, but in some places, at least, the crafts soon developed. It is very probable that the great majority of the articles classical writers mention as being made in Laconia, like iron tools and weapons, woollen cloth, shoes and furniture, were made by artisans settled in the perioecic cities. The Spartans occupied themselves only with warlike pursuits and the administration of the state, and left the cultivation of their land and the running of their households to the helots. The perioeci also engaged in trade, as can be understood from the words of Xenophon's *Constitution of the Lacedaemonians* (7, 5), where he declares that Lycurgus forbade the perioeci the 'wrongful acquiring of riches'. Indeed, some of the perioecic cities, like the port of Gytheum in southern Laconia, were well placed for trading and overseas contacts.

The development of craft production and trade naturally led to social differentiation, at least in some of the perioecic cities. This corresponds with those passages in classical authors that refer to 'beautiful and good' as well as 'noble' perioeci. It is not surprising that the perioecic cities maintained their loyalty to the Spartan state. When the great helot rebellion broke out in the sixties of the fifth century, there were only two perioecic cities that joined the rebels, one of them in Messenia, in a region bordering on the central part where the helots were settled. The location of the other city is not known, but it is sometimes also thought to have been in this area. On the other hand, there seem to have been perioeci involved in Cinadon's unsuccessful rising in the early fourth century, and in this connection they, too, are listed among the discriminated groups who hated the privileged Spartans.

Compared with the perioeci, and especially with the helots, the Spartans formed but a minority within the state. If they were to keep power in their own hands, they had to maintain the military way of life they had brought with them when they invaded Laconia. Some of the curious features of Spartan family life were indeed of ancient origin. In antiquity the freedom enjoyed by the women of Sparta was proverbial, and unlike the girls of other Greek cities, Spartan maidens took part in physical training. The men were obliged to attend communal meals (the *syssitia*, or *phiditia*) contributing produce from their allotted land. Their food was proverbially very simple. These communal meals can be regarded as surviving traces of the 'men's houses' known among some primitive peoples. There are also analogical phenomena in Greece and particularly in Crete.

Special care was taken over the upbringing of Spartan boys, who were subjected to systematic training from the age of eight years, in age-groups each of which had a special name. Adolescents from fourteen to twenty passed through a similar system of education. Here, too, we find many analogous institutions among the primitive tribes of Australia, Africa and North America.

Although the boys and youths of Sparta spent most of their time in physical training, they also learned to sing warlike songs and to recite verse inciting them to courage and manliness. They were expected to live very abstemiously, and to be ready to endure hardship and suffering. They were permitted to steal food, but the punishment for being caught was severe. Their training had but a single goal — military service. At twenty the youth was admitted to the society of the men, and allowed to marry, but since his prime duty was defence of his country, he remained bound by the strictest discipline. Not until the age of thirty was the men's regime lightened. As Plutarch observed in his *Life of Lycurgus* (25), Spartans below the age of thirty were not allowed to frequent the *agora* ('marketplace'), but had to send their friends to buy what they needed for their household. It was considered blameworthy, even for older men, to be too engrossed in their own affairs instead of directing their activities to the welfare of the state.

We are acquainted with many of these features of Spartan society from the writings of classical authors and later accounts, but it is clear that the regime thus depicted must have been formed in the archaic period of Greek history. Some of the dispensations continued ancient traditions going back to the time when the Dorian invaders arrived in

Laconia and laid the foundations of the Spartan (Lacedaemonian) state.

In Sparta, as in many other regions settled by the Dorians, three Dorian phylae are attested: the Hylleis, the Dymanes and the Pamphyloi; it was not until later that distribution of citizens was carried out on a territorial basis. Four settlements sprang up on Spartan territory: Pitana, Mesoa, Cynosoura and Limnae. Close to the little hill on which the Spartan acropolis was raised lay Pitana and Mesoa, where the earliest Protogeometric shards have been found. The other two settlements must also have been very old; the temple of Artemis Orthia at Limnae, close to the Eurotas (*limne* means 'stagnant water', 'marsh'), was probably founded right at the beginning of the ninth century. Sparta kept its rural character for a long time, not becoming a walled city until Hellenistic times. All four settlements, as well as the nearby one of Amyclae, formed part of the city of Sparta for administrative purposes. This was after Sparta had subjugated Amyclae, an occurrence for which there are no reliable reports, but which probably took place in the first half of the eighth century. It would seem that a compromise solution was found, since the Achaeans of Amyclae became full citizens of the Spartan state.

When the Spartans had become the masters of the whole of the valley of the Eurotas they were able to turn their attention to the internal organization of the state. This found expression in what is called the 'Rhetra of Lycurgus'. Spartan tradition had it that the state had been founded by Lycurgus, who was said to be the author of many measures and institutions. Classical writers were already divided in their ideas as to when Lycurgus lived, placing him at various dates between the Dorian invasion of Laconia and the eighth century, while it was even suggested that there had been two men of that name in Sparta, at two different periods. It is therefore not surprising to find Plutarch, in his introduction to the *Life of Lycurgus*, declaring that 'it is not possible to make a single statement (about him) that is not disputable', since reports of his life and work were contradictory and there was least agreement of all about when he lived. A number of varied hypotheses have been put forward in modern times to explain Lycurgus; some scholars believe him to have been a god connected with the cult of Zeus or Apollo, others that a reformer active in Sparta in the sixth century took the name in order to lend greater weight to his measures. There have been unconvincing attempts, more recently, to show that he was a historical person. All we can do is admit that there is no positive proof that Lycurgus ever really existed.

In classical antiquity it was believed that the 'Rhetra of Lycurgus' was an oracle which the Spartan reformer had brought from Delphi. As given by Plutarch (*Lycurgus* 6) the text presents many antiquated expressions, and today it is generally accepted that it is a document dating from early Greek history and reflecting the basic features of Spartan society. The English translation reads: 'To found a sanctuary of Zeus Syllanius and Athena Syllania, arrange the phylae and *obae*, establish as the *gerusia* thirty including the *archagetae*, hold the *apella* from season to season, between Babyka and Knakion, thus put proposals and decline to do so. The *damos* shall have the right of refusal[?] and the power.' In the manuscript of Plutarch's text the last sentence is damaged, and there are several proposals for restitution. The meaning of the other clauses of the Rhetra is not clear either, and there are varying interpretations of individual expressions as well as of the whole document. It is evident from the commentary in which Plutarch attempted to explain the different parts of the Rhetra, that even in ancient times there was confusion on many points.

Although there have been ingenious etymological suggestions, the attributes of Zeus and Athena have not been satisfactorily explained, but it is very probable that both cults formed part of the ancient Dorian tradition. The clause about the phylae and *obae* concerns the organization of the citizens of Sparta. The phylae seem to be the three Dorian phylae of the Hylleis, Dymanes and Pamphyloi. Besides the phylae there were *phratries*, and according to the sources there were twenty-seven of them, which means that each phyle was divided into nine phratries. The obae are attested in epigraphical evidence dating from Hellenistic and Roman times, when they were identified with the settlements which went to make up Sparta, and which were also known by the term *komai* ('villages'). In spite of attempts by some scholars to link the obae with a division of the population along tribal lines in the early history of Sparta, it is likely that at the time the Rhetra was drawn up the obae were already units of local division of the territory of Sparta, including the settlement of Amyclae.

The next clause of the Rhetra concerns the *gerusia* (council of elders), and the figure of thirty members thereof; there were already differing views as to the reason for this number, among ancient writers. There can be no doubt that the council of the elders already existed in Sparta, and that the Rhetra did no more than fix the number of its members. It is most probable that the explanation is to be found in the preceding lines of the text, specifying that the Spartans are to be organized both according to their phylae and according to the obae, of which there were five. The number of *gerontes* (members of the gerusia) was probably so decided as to correspond both to the tribal and the local divisions of the people of Sparta. In this manner the individual phylae and the obae would have the same number of representatives in the gerusia.

The *archagetae* (supreme commanders) were of special standing among the gerontes. We learn from Plutarch's commentary that in the Rhetra this term is used for the basileis. There were two kings in Sparta, chosen from two tribes, the Agiads and the Eurypontids; we have no reliable information about the emergence of this diarchy. Although Spartan tradition ascribed greater respect for the Agiads, I do not accept those theories that suppose a single Spartan king at some period. It was primarily in the military sphere that the royal function was paramount in Sparta. Even in ancient times, the institution of two kings was considered a stabilizing factor in the Spartan regime.

The next clause of the Rhetra deals with the popular assembly, the *apella*. We know from later reports that the apella met once a month, and thus the term 'from season to season' was usually taken to mean that the Rhetra instituted regular meetings of all the citizens of

Sparta. The place where these meetings were to be held was also set by the Rhetra, but even in classical antiquity the topographical indications were already incomprehensible.

The remainder of the Rhetra cannot be clearly understood, particularly the last clause, where the text is not sound. Complicated speculation has evolved round this clause, but it is highly probable that the clause gave the gerusia the right to place proposals before the apella, and to bring their deliberations to an end, and that the people of Sparta (*damos*), i.e. Spartan citizens with full powers, had the possibility of expressing an opinion on the proposals set before the apella, and determining whether they should be accepted or not.

The Rhetra combined the ancient tribal distribution of the Spartans with a territorial distribution which was established as soon as the Dorian tribes settled the territory of Sparta, and completed when they overran the settlement of Amyclae and annexed it to Sparta. The Rhetra set the number of members of the gerusia accordingly, and at the same time determined the competency and the powers of the apella.

The Spartans were not content to have conquered the valley of the Eurotas, and turned their attention to more conquests of fertile land. The most tempting goal was the fertile valley of the river Pamisus in neighbouring Messenia. Although this region is separated from Laconia by the Taygetus range, rearing to a height of 2,400 metres (7,900ft), the Spartans raided it frequently, bringing about a state of war between Sparta and Messenia. The conflict between Sparta and Messenia is described in detail in the third book of Pausanias' *Description of Greece*. The author drew on histories of Messenia which were written in the fourth and third centuries BC, not long after Messenia became independent after centuries of subjugation. His sources are therefore biased in favour of the Messenian side, traditionally showing in a heroic light the Messenian resistance to Spartan expansion, and wreathing the protagonists in legendary exploits. All we know for certain is that there were two Spartan-Messenian wars in the archaic period, the first probably being fought in the second half of the eighth century. In the end, in spite of a long and successful defence against Sparta, and aid from Arcadia and Sicyon (if ancient tradition is to be believed), the Messenians were overcome by the forces of Sparta, aided by those of Corinth. The valley of the Pamisus was overrun by the Spartans, who made the Messenian population helots and divided the land between themselves as they had previously done in Laconia.

It would appear that the kings and other Spartan aristocrats took the lion's share of the loot from Messenia. There is some evidence of conflicts within Spartan society after the first Messenian War, and one of the consequences was perhaps the founding of the colony of Taras (Tarentum) at the end of the eighth century. This seems to be the context into which the rider to the Rhetra fits; Plutarch testifies that it was added by two kings of Sparta when the people distorted and amended the proposals put before the apella. The rider is said to have established that 'if the damos speaks crooked, the gerontes and the archagetae shall refuse it[?]'. This meant a considerable strengthening of the position of the kings and the other gerontes against the apella.

Later tradition tells of conflicts in Sparta in the first half of the seventh century; the lyric poet Terpander of Lesbos is said to have had such power over the Spartans that he not only won the contest during the festival of the Carneia at the time of the twenty-sixth Olympic Games (some time between 676 and 673 BC), but persuaded them to drop their differences. Despite the legendary character of this account, it shows that internal conflicts were known to exist in Sparta. There is evidence of such conflict in both Herodotus and Thucydides, although it is not clear how their comments are to be understood, or the historical dating of their evidence.

It would appear that the Spartans did not enjoy the loot from the invasion of Messenia on an equal basis, which led to tension between the aristocrats and the ordinary people. The poet Alcman, who was writing about the middle of the seventh century BC in Sparta, and who was thought to have been a native either of Sardes in Asia Minor or of Sparta itself, commented in one of the fragments of his verse which have survived, that the people of Sparta had to put up with simple, badly prepared food. Discontent with existing conditions was marked during the second war between Sparta and the Messenians, which probably broke out about this time. In his *Politics* (5, 1306b–1307a) Aristotle said that some of the Spartans had suffered as a result of the war and therefore 'demanded that the land should be redistributed'. He gives the poet Tyrtaeus as his authority for this, the poet whose militant verse roused the Spartans to fight the Messenians who had taken to arms to win back their freedom. It took all the Spartans could do, for a long time, to get the better of the rebels. Unlike the first Messenian War, in which the fighting seems to have followed the tradition we know from the Homeric epics, the second Messenian War seems to have seen the introduction of new tactics. Man-to-man encounters between aristocratic protagonists gave way to battles in which, according to the poems of Tyrtaeus, the main burden was borne by the closed phalanx of the hoplites. This is borne out by the lead votive figures of hoplites found in the temple of Artemis Orthia, and dating from the second half of the seventh century. The Spartan soldiers seem to have been aware of their power, and to have demanded a redistribution of the land. The aristocracy may have been forced to give the common people of Sparta a greater share of the loot in Messenia.

The rebellion of the Messenian helots brought home to the Spartans the fact that the stability of their country could only be ensured if all the citizens stood together. To achieve this unity the role of the ephorate was decisive. It was not so ancient an institution as the kingship, the gerusia or the apella, and was not derived from the Dorian tribal institutions. The five-member council of ephors corresponded more to the division of Sparta into obae, and Spartan tradition dated the ephorate from the middle of the eighth century, the period when the annexation of the settlement of Amyclae brought the unification of Sparta to an end. It was not until after the second Messenian War, however, that the institution became of major importance. The ephors were elected annually, from the ranks of the citizens of Sparta, and it was their responsibility to see that the laws were kept and that the representatives of the state, including the kings, did their job properly; they thus became the most powerful officials in the country. The Spartans named the year after the senior ephor, the eponym (*onyma*, *onoma*, meaning name). The ephors were the guardians of the traditions of Sparta and tried to strengthen the unity of all its citizens. Some scholars believe that Chilon, who held office in the middle of the sixth century (probably in the year 556/5) and was honoured as one of the Seven Sages in the Greek tradition, was particularly deserving of note in this respect.

It was not until the sixth century BC that the state (*polis*) of Sparta attained its final form, but from that time onwards the provisions of Lycurgus were strictly adhered to. In particular, great care was taken not to allow bad influences and evil example to penetrate Sparta from the outside world, an artificial isolation which had a deleterious effect on the evolution of Spartan culture. The work of Spartan artists and craftsmen equalled that of other civilized Greek cities during the seventh century and the first half of the sixth, but thereafter the standard fell. The same tendency can be seen in literature and in music, while the number of victors in the Olympic Games who came from Sparta fell sharply after the middle of the sixth century, although Spartans had been outstanding at the Games in earlier times.

Sparta had become one of the greatest and most powerful Greek states, ruling over Laconia and Messenia, including the perioecic settlements, and pushing her frontiers even further north after defeating Argos in the middle of the sixth century. The people of many cities of southern Greece were bound to Sparta by treaties of alliance, giving Sparta hegemony within the Peloponnesian League which embraced the whole of the peninsula, except for Argos and Achaea. The helot problem, however, remained the Achilles heel of the Spartan state.

Ancient writers had already likened the institutions of Sparta to those of the Dorian settlements in Crete; indeed the Dorians are mentioned in the *Odyssey* itself (19, 177). This is a reflection of the times in which the epics came into being, however, and cannot be taken as evidence of Dorian settlement of Crete before they arrived in the Peloponnese. The names of the three Dorian phylae (the Hylleis, Dymanes and Pamphyloi) are found in numerous inscriptions from central and eastern Crete, dating from Hellenistic times. It is clear that in Crete the Dorians found themselves obliged to come to terms with the earlier settlers to a much greater degree than on the Greek mainland. The ethnic structure of the island had been complex even in Minoan times. The Dorian influence was uppermost particularly in the towns of central Crete, like Knossos, Axos, Lyttos and Gortyn, which dominated the plateau south of the Mount Ida range.

In his *Politics* (2, 1271b–1272) Aristotle compared the Spartan constitution with that of Crete and came to the conclusion that the Spartans had taken over many of the features of their system from the Cretans. This view derived from a consciousness that there had been an old Cretan civilization, and indeed Aristotle refers explicitly to laws laid down by Minos. In Crete as in Sparta the council of the elders (gerontes) was very important. The rank of basileus was known only in earlier times, being abolished in the Cretan cities later on. The executive power was in the hands of a council of ten *kosmoi*, but unlike the ephors of Sparta, the kosmoi were elected not from the whole citizen body, but only from certain families. The council of elders (gerontes) was formed of men who had served as kosmoi, and according to Aristotle comprised the same number of members as in Sparta.

These conditions seem to have applied only in the larger cities, like Knossos or Gortyn, but naturally the institutions were not identical in all respects all over the island. An interesting inscription probably dating from the end of the seventh century, found in Dreros in the east of Crete, throws light on the institutions on the island. It reveals that a citizen who had served as a *kosmos* could not be re-elected until after ten years had passed, and that there were penalties for breaking that rule. The inscription also refers to a 'council of twenty', presumably the council of elders. The whole text was formulated as a decree of the *polis*, and is in fact one of the earliest examples of the use of the term in an official inscription.

Communal meals are also attested in Crete, and the term used for them, *andreia* (*aner*, genitive *andros*, man), which was also occasionally used in Sparta, shows that this was a custom dating from the times of the 'men's houses'. Unlike the Spartans, however, the Cretan Dorians did not contribute the produce of their own land to the communal meals, but financed them from public funds. In addition, it appears that women and children took part.

Careful attention was paid to the upbringing of children. Small boys were already trained to be hardy and were obliged not only to look after themselves, but to wait on the grown men as well. The older boys were organized in groups for physical training and also, according to the historian Ephorus, of the fourth century BC, for learning 'their letters and songs in the ancient modes, and some forms of music' (in Strabo 10, 482). The boys' teams engaged in military contests to the accompaniment of the lyre and pipes.

The complicated ethnic situation and differences between the individual Cretan cities led to the emergence of varying forms of land tenure. As far as we can judge, there was communal land in Crete side by side with the allotments of land granted to each citizen for cultivation. In the cities of Crete, as in Sparta, it was the earlier stratum of the population which worked the land, after they had been subjugated by the Dorian invaders. Those working on communal land were called *mnoitai*. The basic unit of land, however, was the civic *klaros* or *oikos*, and the peasants bound to this land were called *klarotai* in classical literature, or sometimes *aphamiotai*. In his account of those people 'in between the freemen and the slaves', quoted earlier, Pollux mentions the Cretan *klarotai* and *mnoitai* among the helots and other groups.

The 'Code of Gortyn' provides us with curious insights into the social structure of the Cretan cities and the legal standing of the different groups of the population. This is an extensive and for the most part well-preserved inscription dating from the first half of the fifth century, but there can be no doubt that many of the clauses of the Code are much older than that. The first part lists the penalties for various offences; these are fines, varying according to the social standing of both accused and victim.

The citizens with full rights were a privileged group in Gortyn. Below them came the *apetairoi*, free men who were not members of the *hetaireiai*, which may have been the equivalent of the Spartan phratries. The fines were heaviest and the damages paid lightest, in the case of the bonded peasants, called *woikees*. The word is derived from the term for the allotment of land (*[w]oikeus* from *[w]oikos*) and corresponds to the term *klarotai* (from *klaros*) commonly used by classical sources. Besides these, the word *dolos* also occurs in the Code of Gortyn (meaning 'a slave'; in the Ionian and Attic dialects it was *doulos*), sometimes apparently in the same sense as *woikeus*, while elsewhere it seems to refer to serfs or perhaps to domestic slaves.

Other clauses of the Code provide for property settlement in cases of marriage, the death of one partner to a marriage, or divorce. The case of children born to an unmarried or divorced woman of the bonded peasant class is also dealt with: the child of an unmarried woman was the property of her father's master, or if her father was no longer alive, of her brothers' master. The child of a divorced woman was to be given to the master of her former husband, and only if that master was not interested did the child revert to her own master. We learn from the text, too, that marriage was possible in Gortyn between slave and free; if a slave moved in with a woman who was free, and married her, their children were born free. If a free woman moved in with a slave, however, their children were born slaves.

Inheritance and adoption play an important part in the clauses of the Gortyn Code, aiming always at preserving the family property intact. The same purpose was behind the regulations about heiresses, defined as women who have 'no father and no brother of the same father'. It was her duty to marry a male relative on her father's side. Similar injunctions are known from other Greek cities.

CHAPTER IV

Greek Colonization and Social Change

In many parts of Greece small states were formed during the archaic period, often described as 'city-states'. The term is not really apposite, however, for although these states usually centred round a city, the rural hinterland was an integral part of them, and often an extensive part. The city-state of Athens, for instance, embraced the whole of Attica, which meant that it also included a number of other settlements, some of which were urban in character. The many perioecic towns in Laconia and later in Messenia were all part of the Spartan (Lacedaemonian) state, while Sparta itself was not a walled city, persisting for long as a conglomeration of four village settlements. Although the city usually served as the administrative and cultural centre of the state, it was agriculture which formed the fundamental economic and social basis of its existence. Only those who owned land could enjoy citizen rights, while only full citizens, in general, were allowed to own land within the city-state.

The Greeks themselves used the term *polis* for this type of state, but especially in earlier usage it, too, had a broader meaning. It is already found in Homer, usually signifying a walled city as distinct from the countryside, but soon came to be the official term for a city-state. One of the earliest instances of this usage comes from Dreros in

Crete, in an inscription which can be dated to the turn of the seventh century BC. The two great thinkers of classical Greece, Plato and Aristotle, have given us a full account of the characteristic features and specific forms of the polis, and something of its history. Their theoretical inferences have led writers on the subject to adopt the Greek term polis for the city-state of Greece.

As we see from Thucydides (2, 15, 6) the Athenians in his day were still using the term polis for the fortified hill which formed the most ancient part of the city. In fact the common word *acropolis* which still denotes this part of the city today, means no more than 'town on a hill' or 'fortified town'. For this reason the connection is sometimes made between the fortified palaces of the Mycenaeans — of which the Athenian acropolis was one — and the cities which later formed the administrative centres of the Greek states. Only in exceptional cases, however, can continuous settlement be proved. It is of course important to note that the economic, social and political conditions in the Mycenaean states were very different from those which evolved in the Greek poleis. In Mycenaean times the state was headed by an all-powerful ruler who managed his palace economy with the help of a bureaucratic apparatus. In the archaic period in Greece, however, a society of a completely novel type emerged, based on the community of the citizens (*koinonia ton politon*). The Greek idea of the state was not based primarily on a unit of territory, but rather on a social unit formed by the citizens. This can be seen, too, in the fact that the Greeks did not as a rule call their states by local names (Athens, Sparta, or Corinth), but used words which stressed the identity of the citizens who made up the state (that is to say, the Athenians, Lacedaemonians, or Corinthians).

The evolution of the Greek city-states (poleis) was a long process. The state of the sources usually allows us to trace the history of the poleis only in bare outline, and with a few exceptions only from the middle of the seventh century BC, so that we are thrown back on hypothetical conclusions. It is difficult to say when the poleis began to take shape, and evolution proceeded at a different pace in different parts of the country, as indeed is normal in the course of history. The individual poleis evolved with specific distinctive features due to their different conditions, some of which have already been mentioned in the previous chapter. A tribal organization persisted in the less developed parts of Greece right into the classical period.

At the time when the Ionians, Aeolians and Dorians were settling the islands of the Aegean and the western shores of Asia Minor, at the end of the eleventh and in the early tenth century, the Greeks were organized in tribes (phylae). The movement to colonize which began in the eighth century, on the other hand, had a new basis. Although traces of the tribal organization can still be seen both in the cities establishing colonies and in the colonies themselves, new elements can be clearly traced which were to become characteristic for the poleis. In general it can be said that the process of formation of the city-states was under way between the eighth and sixth century BC, that is to say during the archaic period of Greek history. It was at this time that Greek colonies began to appear at various points along the shores of the Mediterranean and then of the Black Sea. These two significant phenomena stand in mutual causal relationship.

In history the word colonization usually denotes the penetration of further territory by a powerful centre, in order to conquer and exploit new regions to enrich the centre and strengthen its influence. This was the motivation, for example, leading to the founding of Roman colonies in Italy in antiquity. The colonies served as bases for the military and political power of Rome. The citizens of the colonies remained Roman citizens and represented Roman interests in the colonized regions.

Greek colonization during the eighth to sixth centuries was of a different character. The Greeks themselves used the word *apoikia* for their colonies. Every citizen had his *oikos* — that is to say, his home and his farm — in his original community; the formation of an apoikia thus meant that a group of citizens moved away and set up their homes elsewhere. When the settlers reached their goal, they would take over the land and divide it among themselves, creating a new citizen community. The apoikia became an independent economic and political unit, the nucleus of a new city-state which then continued to grow and take shape in its new setting, free of the influence of the city left behind.

Certain traditional bonds between the original city and its colonies were maintained, however. In Tarentum, for instance, the cult of the same gods and heroes as in the home state of Sparta is attested. When the Corcyraeans set out to found the colony of Epidamnus (later Dyrrhachium, now the Albanian port of Durrës), they requested their 'mother-city' of Corinth to send someone to lead the settlers to their new home. Similarly when the citizens of Megara Hyblaea in Sicily were founding Selinus, they asked for a citizen from their 'mother-city' of Megara in Greece to head the settlement. Both these instances are also illustrations of the fact that the colonies were independent communities which in their turn could establish their own colonies.

Citizens setting out to found a colony were given not only what they needed for the voyage, but all that was necessary for them to start life in their new home. That included arms and equipment (including tools and implements) and also seed. It was usual for the future settlers to be excluded from the ranks of the citizens from the moment they set out from their native shore, and to acquire new citizenship as they founded a colony based on land ownership. Naturally it was mostly young people who joined these expeditions, to make a new home when their native community could not provide enough opportunities for them, or when they had some other cause for dissatisfaction. It was usual to place a man from one of the aristocratic families at the head of the expedition, and in earlier times the title *archegetes* was used (Ionian form of the title given to the kings in the Rhetra of Lycurgus). It probably dates from the time of the great migration after the decline of the Mycenaean civilization, after the arrival of the Dorian and north-western tribes in Greece. An expedition making for unknown or little explored shores was a risky undertaking, and called for military leadership. Later on, the man at the head of such an expedition was called *oikistes*. Sometimes several cities joined together to form a colonizing expedition, and then one of them would assume the functions of the 'mother-city'.

Relations between the Greek colonies and the local inhabitants varied greatly from place to place. The settlements formed by Greek colonists in the traditionally civilized regions of the Near East, in Syria and in Egypt, had a special character; hence the Greeks drew ideas which further advanced the economic and cultural life of the Greek world. Elsewhere the roles were reversed. The Greek colonies on the south-west coast of Italy, for example, introduced technical and agricultural skills to regions controlled by the Etruscans; in this way the Etruscans — and through them the Romans — acquired the alphabet. The inhabitants of the eastern shores of Sicily rapidly and spontaneously absorbed Hellenic influences. The Greek colonists in some places had to defend the land they had occupied, and relations between them and the local people were not always friendly. The opposition to Greek colonization was particularly strong on the northern shores of the Aegean, which had been settled by Thracians.

Greek colonization began during the eighth century, at a very favourable time. The Phoenicians had reached the western fringes of the Mediterranean and the northern coast of Africa, founding Kart-Hadasht (New City) there at the end of the ninth century, the settlement which later became famous under its Latinized name of Carthage; they were now exposed to strong pressure because of Assyrian expansion into Syria. The true cause of the Greek move to found colonies is of course to be sought in the internal situation in Greece. The evil times which had followed the fall of the Mycenaean civilization, and the disruption caused by the migrations, had all been overcome, and the Greeks were moving towards new economic prosperity and advances in civilization. In Al-Mina they had not only come into contact with the traditions of oriental cultures and seen their wealth, but had learned of the successful voyages of Phoenician sailors to strange lands on the western shores of the Mediterranean. It is not impossible that, before the Greeks began founding their colonies, individual explorers, and especially merchants and crafts-men, had already travelled to these lands. The archaeological evidence, particularly finds of Greek pottery, agree on the whole with the account given by classical authors, however, and it is very rare indeed that a Greek presence is attested for a time previous to the establishment of the colony.

As the Greeks began to broaden their horizons and embrace the whole of the Mediterranean world, an awareness of a common culture and national feeling grew up. Through contacts with strange lands and peoples, the idea of Hellenic civilization was formed. The Greeks realized that although they came of different tribes and spoke various dialects, and although their religious ideas were markedly diverse, they nevertheless formed an ethnic entity distinct from the alien 'barbarian' (i.e. linguistically incomprehensible) surroundings. The Homeric epics strengthened the Greek cultural traditions and unified the religious ideas of the Greeks; a common mythology grew up, and formed part of their view of their history. Later accounts place the beginnings of the Olympic Games at this time, too, dating the first in 776 BC. Although the date is purely imaginary, archaeological evidence goes to prove that the shrine of Zeus at Olympia in Elis gradually acquired more than a local significance during the eighth century, becoming a religious, cultural and agonistic (i.e. athletic) centre for all the Greeks. Every four years athletic contests were held here, as well as musical and literary competitions. Other religious centres also grew in importance, especially the shrine of Apollo at Delphi, which often sanctified the Greek pioneers setting out to found a new home. This function was performed by another shrine dedicated to Apollo when Greek expeditions set out for the Black Sea; the Ionians in Asia Minor set up a shrine and oracle of Apollo at Didyma, about 15 km (9 miles) south of Miletus.

In the nineteenth century scholars varied in their view of the reasons for Greek colonization, some stressing the purely mercantile incentives, while others saw it as analogous to the aims of the capitalist states of their own time, transferring to the ancient Greek scene the typical phenomena of modern colonialism, the fight for sources of raw materials, for markets in which they could sell industrial produce, and for spheres of influence. Others, in their earnest endeavour to combat these anachronistic ideas, denied that trade had anything to do with the establishment of the Greek colonies. The discussion which surrounded the problem of why the Greeks founded colonies was itself one aspect of the argument about the very nature of antique civilization; those who in the interests of modernity exaggerated the importance to the Greek cities of trade and craft production took issue with those who held that the economy of ancient Greece was based on self-contained economic units (*oikoi*) which produced enough for their own needs and therefore did not have to develop trade relations. The latest evidence unearthed by archaeologists on the sites of many Greek colonies and a closer knowledge of the nature of the city-states suggest that there is no justification for over-emphasizing either type of colony — 'agrarian' or 'trading'. In the early stages of colonization, in particular, the demographic factor was of prime importance. In Greece, where the area of land suitable for cultivation was limited, and agriculture still at a low level of productivity, the land became overcrowded relatively early. The land lots were not always sufficient to feed all the members of the family, and younger sons, in particular, welcomed the opportunity to found a home of their own, even in some far-away place. Land ownership was always of great importance in the founding of a colony. At the same time it would be wrong to underestimate the mercantile aspect of colonization, especially in the relations which developed between the new settlers and the local inhabitants. It must also be remembered that the move towards colonization was going on at the same time as the city-states were forming, a time of social upheaval and political instability. Tensions grew in the Greek cities, and dissatisfied citizens sometimes sought an outlet in emigration.

Among the cities which were most active in the drive to colonize were Chalcis and Eretria on the island of Euboea; the Chalcidians were particularly agile. Euboean pioneers founded the colony of Cumae (Cyme) on the northern shore of the Gulf of Naples, probably about the middle of the eighth century. According to ancient tradition as recorded by Strabo (5,243) and Livy (8,22), the Euboean settlers first landed on the island of Pithecusae (now Ischia) and only transferred to the mainland later, where they founded Cyme.

Scepticism about this account has been cleared away by the results of archaeological research on Ischia, which has proved that Greeks were settled there before the middle of the eighth century.

It is interesting to note that the first Greek settlement in the west was founded in the immediate vicinity of Etruscan-controlled territory, and the Greek influence on Etruscan life was very marked from the end of the eighth century onwards. Greek Geometric pottery has been found on Etruscan sites and later strata have yielded pottery with oriental-style motifs. Probably at that time, too, Euboean settlers introduced the Etruscans to goods from Near East workshops, for they have been found in late eighth-century strata in Pithecusae and in Etruria itself. Influences from Greece and from the Near East are very marked in Etruscan art itself, while the script taken over by the Etruscans from the Greeks used signs identical with some of the letters in the alphabet used on Euboea. As we have already seen, one of the earliest surviving documents written in Greek — the inscription on a cup — was found in Pithecusae. It is most likely that the Greeks bartered their works of art for metals, both tin and copper which they needed to make bronze, and iron. The primary interest of the settlers, of course, was to cultivate the fertile soil of Italy, and there can be no doubt that agriculture was the principal source of subsistence for the people of Cyme as of other Euboean settlements.

The Chalcidians soon moved towards the eastern coast of Sicily, founding the colony of Naxos round the middle of the eighth century and Zancle on the straits between Sicily and Italy, in the thirties; at the beginning of the fifth century the latter was renamed Messana (now Messina). There were citizens from the island of Samos among the settlers there. Not long afterwards the colony of Rhegium (now Reggio di Calabria) was founded on the other side of the straits, in Italy, and among the settlers here, besides Chalcidians from Euboea and Zancle, there were Messenians who had left their country after its defeat by Sparta in the First Messenian War. Systematic archaeological research in the hinterland of the Euboean colonies leads us to conclude that the settlers lived on good terms with the original inhabitants of eastern Sicily, the Sicels. All the evidence suggests that the Sicels living near Naxos and Leontini (which was founded from Naxos), for instance, absorbed the Greek way of life and gradually became Hellenized.

Chalcis and Eretria were not the only Greek cities to send pioneers to the shores of Sicily and southern Italy. In the second half of the eighth century Megara was founded, not far from Leontini; to distinguish it from the 'mother-city' of Megara it was usually called Megara Hyblaea. The colony had only a slight hinterland and was soon overshadowed by Syracuse, which had been founded from Corinth, and which possessed an excellent port in a bay, partly enclosed by the island of Ortygia. It was here that the Sicels had a settlement which had to give way to the Greek colony, and as we noted in the previous chapter, some of the peasants, the Kyllyrioi, stood in a dependent relationship reminiscent of that of the Spartan helots. The colonists of Syracuse systematically extended their sphere of influence. Like Syracuse, Gela, founded at the beginning of the seventh century on the southern coast of Sicily by colonists from Rhodes and Crete, had taken over land that was inhabited, pushing the people further inland. Here it was the Sicans (another native Sicilian tribe) who were dispossessed. Recent archaeological study has suggested that here, too, there was lively contact between the Greeks and the local population at first, but later hostility seems to have arisen, resulting in the destruction of a number of Sican settlements.

At the beginning of the sixth century the people of Gela founded Acragas (now Agrigento) on the site of a Sican settlement, but already in the second half of the seventh century a colony had arisen at Selinus, further west along the southern coast, founded by citizens of Megara Hyblaea. Selinus soon achieved great prosperity, and the temples which have survived, with their ornament, are among the finest examples of archaic Greek art. At the end of the sixth century the earliest of a series of temples was built in Acragas, which soon held its own with its western neighbour both in trade and culture, and completely overshadowed the 'mother-city' of Gela. One of the last sites in the Sicilian area to be settled by the Greeks were the Lipari Islands.

Colonization went on no less actively along the southern coast of Italy. Besides the Euboean colonies we have already mentioned as the spearhead of Greek influence in the region, one of the most important Greek colonies was that of Taras (gen. Tarantos, now Taranto). It was founded towards the end of the eighth century by Spartans; according to legend they were *parthenioi* (from *parthenos* meaning 'virgin' or 'unmarried woman'), the illegitimate sons of Spartan mothers who were dissatisfied with their underprivileged standing in the state and plotted to change it. They were forced to leave Sparta and seek new homes. The historical basis of this legend is not known, but as we have seen in the chapter on Sparta, the founding of Taras seems to have been motivated by conditions within Sparta after the First Messenian War. Archaeological evidence suggests that at first Sparta had practically nothing to do with its only colony, and not until the sixth century do we find imported Spartan pottery, and signs that some of the Spartan religious ideas and practices were maintained in Taras. The colony possessed an excellent port, still one of the best in southern Italy today, and fertile land for cultivation.

South of Taras, settlers from Achaea in the Peloponnese had founded Sybaris somewhat earlier. Here, too, the soil was suitable for grain and for vineyards. Sybaris maintained lively contact with the south-west Italian coast, and seems to have been instrumental in the contacts between the Etruscans and Miletus in Asia Minor. The wealth and luxury of Sybaris was proverbial, and the cause of jealous hostility among her neighbours. Towards the end of the sixth century internal strife weakened the colony of Sybaris which was then overthrown by her most formidable rival, Croton, a colony founded somewhat later, also by settlers from Achaea.

When Sybaris fell, her colonies nevertheless survived, among them Metapontum (Metapontion), founded to the west of Taras at the turn of the eighth century, and the somewhat later founded Poseidonia (known as Paestum in Roman times), to the south of Cyme. The prosperity of Poseidonia is attested today by the ruins of sixth-century fortifications and of two temples dating from the same century. In the middle of the fifth century a temple was built to Hera, which is now one of the best-preserved examples of Greek architecture. Recent excavations have revealed a sacred hill dedicated to Hera, about 13 kilometres (8 miles) north-west of the colony proper, where the remains of temple buildings of the archaic period have been uncovered.

Greek pottery dating from the turn of the eighth century has been unearthed on Sicel sites on the southern coast of Italy, probably the work of Greek potters who had settled there. At the beginning of the second quarter of the seventh century the Locri from central Greece founded a colony in the region which was called Locri. From here they extended their influence to the western coast as well. The Greek colonies in southern Italy had a fertile agricultural hinterland, and most of them also flourished on trade with other regions, including the more distant parts of Italy.

As in Sicily, the colonies in southern Italy propagated the advantages of Greek civilization among the local population; at the same time they were an integral part of the Greek world and contributed significantly to its progress in all spheres. The flourishing south Italian colonies merited the name of Greater Greece (Megale Hellas) given to the region.

The archaeological material yielded by the Sicilian and south Italian sites has produced Corinthian pottery in the early strata. At the time when the Greeks were open to eastern influences, the civilization of Syria and Phoenicia, it was in the work of Corinthian potters that this was most evident; towards the end of the eighth century they were replacing the Geometric style with a new one known in the literature as the Proto-Corinthian. The Corinthians also enjoyed the reputation of skilled sailors. Thucydides (1, 13) tells how 'the Corinthians, it is said, were the first sailors to adopt a system very like the one used today, and the first Greek triremes were built at Corinth'. We learn further that one Ameinocles of Corinth built three vessels of this type (i.e. with three rows of oars one above the other) for the people of the island of Samos, as long ago as 'three hundred years before this war ended'. This means that Thucydides dates the first successes of the Corinthian sailors and boat-builders to the end of the eighth century.

The Corinthians founded only one colony in Sicily, choosing for it a site that offered one of the finest natural harbours. Syracuse later became the richest and most powerful city of the island. Part of the expedition which set out for the Sicilian shore in the thirties of the eighth century — so the account runs — settled on the island of Corcyra (modern Corfu). The Corinthians are said to have fought settlers from Euboean Eretria who were already there, and forced them to move away. The colony then became another important Corinthian settlement. The Corinthian tradition can be clearly seen in the early archaeological material from the site. The traditional ties between Corcyra and the 'mother-city' came into play, as described earlier, when the former asked for an *oikistes* from Corinth before setting out to found the colony of Epidamnus in the second half, or towards the end, of the seventh century. Relations between the two were not of the best, however, and Thucydides commented that 'the first sea battle ever to be fought was, as far as we know, that between the Corinthians and the Corcyrans' which took place 'about 260 years' before the end of the Peloponnesian War, i.e. before the middle of the seventh century. The Corinthians ensured safe contacts with the west by building a chain of settlements stretching from the Isthmus of Corinth to the Ionian Sea.

From the second half of the sixth century the Greeks also began to make contact with the Italian coast across the Adriatic, where a group of Etruscan towns had sprung up. Excavation of the ancient port of Spina, carried out in the 1950s, has revealed surprising finds; the port lay in the lagoon region south of the mouth of the Po, and finds of Attic pottery show that it was founded as early as the archaic period, although it was at the height of its prosperity in classical times. Spina was an important trading centre where Greek settlers lived side by side with the Etruscans and the local Veneti.

Greek expansion did not stop at the shores of the Ionian, Adriatic and Tyrrhenian Seas, but went to the westernmost regions of the

Mediterranean. Here the Greeks carried on the tradition of the Phoenician sailors. Herodotus (4, 152) tells of a ship from Samos, owned by one Kolaios, which set out some time in the second half of the seventh century, from the island of Plataea off the Libyan coast, making for Egypt. An east wind drove her in the opposite direction, and so 'as the wind did not die down, they sailed between the Pillars of Heracles (i.e. the Straits of Gibraltar) and with the help of the gods sailed to Tartessus.' Tartessus, the site of which has not been reliably determined, was famed in ancient times for her wealth, drawn from trade in metals. At the end of the second millennium BC Tartessus was already said to have a lively trade with the Phoenicians. According to Herodotus, the sailors from Samos made a great profit from their chance voyage; they had a great bowl of bronze made from one tenth of their gains, and presented it to the temple of the goddess Hera, on a massive stand.

Elsewhere (1,163) Herodotus links the earliest voyages to the western Mediterranean with the people of the Ionian city of Phocaea, who 'discovered the Adriatic, Tyrrhenian and Iberian regions as well as Tartessus'. Archaeologists have found isolated examples of seventh century Greek pottery at some points along the south coast of France, particularly around the mouth of the Rhône. These early contacts may have been made from Euboean colonies in southern Italy, but before long the Ionians from Asia Minor appeared on the scene; Massalia was the first fixed Greek settlement in the area (the Marseilles of today), founded about the year 600 BC by settlers from Phocaea.

There was lively trade between Massalia and the immediate Ligurian hinterland, and even as far as the regions of the Late Hallstatt culture. The work of Greek potters and metalworkers found its way up the valleys of the Rhône and the Sâone, far into the domains of the Celts. One of the most important sites where Greek imports have been found is the *oppidum* at Mont Lassois in the upper reaches of the Seine (not far from Châtillon-sur-Seine). In the second half of the last century a bronze cauldron on a tripod was found in this region; it is the product of a Greek workshop, dating from the first half of the sixth century BC. In 1953 this was followed by the discovery of a magnificent grave site near Vix, where a Celtic princess was buried. Among the finds was a bronze *krater* ('wine vessel'), 164 cm high (5ft 4½ins), weighing over 4 cwt and decorated with a frieze in low relief, depicting a battle scene. It probably dates from the last quarter of the sixth century. This remarkable example of the high degree of skill of Greek artists working in metal seems to have been specially commissioned; letters on each of the separate parts of the vessel suggest that the Greek master craftsman put it together on the spot. Other Greek imports have been found in Switzerland, in the upper Danube valley, and as far away as southern Sweden, where a bronze cauldron from a Greek workshop has been discovered.

A marble *thesaurus* ('treasury') set up in Delphi in the sixth century by the citizens of Massalia testifies to the colony's prosperity. In the second quarter of the century the Massalians founded the settlement of Emporion (now Ampurias, close to the French-Spanish border) on the north-east coast of Spain; the name itself (*emporion* means 'market') suggests that it was primarily a trading colony. About the same time the Phocaeans founded Alalia on Corsica, thus coming into direct contact with the Etruscans. At first their relations seem to have been friendly enough, but later conflicts arose, growing into open hostility. Herodotus (1, 165-6) says that the trouble arose when new settlers from Phocaea arrived in Alalia, because they resented Persian domination of their home city. 'When they arrived in Corsica they lived with the earlier settlers for five years, and built shrines there. Because they robbed and looted among all the neighbouring peoples, however, the Etruscans and the Carthaginians made war on them together . . .'

Hostility between the Greeks and the Carthaginians was of long standing, dating from the colonization of Sicily by the Greeks, where the interests of the two clashed. Tension was particularly high during the seventies of the sixth century, when settlers from Rhodes and Cnidus tried in vain to found a colony on the western shores of the island. Driven off by the Carthaginians, they finally settled in the Lipari Islands.

Bronze figurine of Spartan girl running,
550–500 BC. Height 11cm (4¼in). National Museum, Athens.

Wall panel from Caere, Etruria,
showing a sphinx, about 570 BC. Height 98cm (3ft 2½in).
British Museum, London.

Clay relief from Syracuse
— perhaps part of the end or side of an altar —
representing the Gorgon with her child, the winged horse Pegasus,
late 7th century BC. Height 56cm (1ft 10in).
Museo Archeologico, Syracuse.

Bronze krater from Vix, France,
with Gorgon, warriors and chariots portrayed
in relief on the handle and neck, 530 – 520 BC. Height 164cm (5ft 4½in).
Musée Archéologique, Châtillon-sur-Seine.

Proto-Corinthian jug (called the Chigi Vase)
from Veii, Etruria, by Macmillan Painter, with friezes
of hoplites in battle (above) and horsemen and hare hunting (below),
about 640–630 BC. Height 26cm (10¼in). Museo Nazionale
di Villa Giulia, Rome.

Above
Metope from the Sicyonian treasury
in Delphi, showing the Dioscuri and the Sons of Aphareus
driving cattle home from a raid, about 560 BC.
Height 58cm (1ft 10¾in). Delphi Museum.
Above left
Proto-Corinthian perfume-flask from Thebes,
with the top moulded as a lion's head and painted friezes showing a fight,
horsemen and a hare hunt, mid-7th century BC. Height 6.35cm (2½in).
British Museum, London.
Far left
Coin (stater) from Miletus, showing a lion with head reverted,
about 575 BC. British Museum, London.
Left
Coin (octodrachm) from Abdera, showing a seated griffin,
about 500–480 BC. Staatliche Museen, Berlin.

Statuette of a priest from Ephesus,
600–550 BC. Height 11.2cm (4½in). Archaeological
Museum, Istanbul.

In the naval battle of Alalia which Herodotus records, and which most probably took place in 540 BC, the Phocaeans defeated the allied forces of the Etruscans and the Carthaginians, but lost most of their ships and a great many men. They therefore decided to leave Alalia and move to Rhegium, from where they founded a colony south of Poseidonia, calling it Hyele (later Elea, the Roman Velia). Massalia continued to extend its influence along the coast, to the west and the east.

Around the year 500 BC there were significant changes in Central Europe; the centres of the Hallstatt culture were deserted, and the La Tène culture evolved in the Celtic sphere, seeking contacts with the Mediterranean across the Alpine passes to northern Italy. Here there was direct contact between Celtic and Etruscan influences, while Massalia lost its connection with that distant hinterland. It still remained the dominant force on the southern French and eastern Spanish coast, however, and founded colonies there at an even later date.

The activities of Greek colonists were no less intense in the eastern Mediterranean. The earliest Greek contacts with the Near East, as we saw in a previous chapter, are attested by archaeological finds at Al-Mina in Syria. Here, of course, the Greeks were in the role of promising pupils rather than the bearers of a new and more advanced civilization, as they were in the west. Excavations at Al-Mina have shown that during the seventh century pottery from Euboea and the Cyclades began to give way to Proto-Corinthian and eastern Greek vases. Some similarity with finds on Aegina suggests that it was the inhabitants of this island who brought Proto-Corinthian pottery to Al-Mina. Eastern Greek pottery is represented on this site by pottery from Rhodes, Chios and the Aeolian region, particularly Lesbos. At the beginning of the sixth century there seems to be a break in continuity, perhaps due to the fall of the Assyrian empire, which was followed by the domination of the New Babylonian empire. Greek contacts with Syria seem to have moved further south, to a settlement at Tell Sukas where eastern Greek, Cypriot and some Athenian pottery has been found.

On the Cilician coast, early archaic Greek pottery has been found at Tarsus. Two colonies on the southern shores of Asia Minor, Soli in Cilicia, west of Tarsus, and Phaselis in Pamphylia, founded by settlers from Rhodes, may date from the beginning of the seventh century. Settlers from the island of Samos also made their home on the Cilician coast. Greek imports have been found in the hinterland of Cilicia, Syria and Palestine. On the other hand, archaic Greek art reveals the influence of impulses from Urartu and Assyria, from Syria and Phoenicia, and from Cyprus.

The Greeks who settled on the west coast of Asia Minor were in lively contact with centres inland. Excavations at Gordium and other cities of ancient Phrygia have yielded imports of eastern Greek and Proto-Corinthian pottery, and show that the Greeks found artistic inspiration here, particularly in metal-working. They also learned the elements of musical theory from the Phrygians (the Phrygian mode) and adopted some religious ideas as well (the worship of Cybele and Attis). Not long after the Greeks had acquired their alphabet, it found its way into Phrygia. In the first half of the seventh century the Phrygian kingdom gave way to pressure from the nomad Cimmerians from north of the Black Sea, and the dominant role in Asia Minor passed to Lydia. The Lydian centre, Sardes, lay in the immediate vicinity of the Ionian region, and this made contact even livelier. The Greeks learned more music from the Lydians (the Lydian mode) and according to Herodotus (1, 94) they also learned to play games there.

Midas king of Phrygia, and Gyges and Croesus of Lydia, found their way into Greek tales and myths, which we know mainly from Herodotus. Midas was notorious for his love of gold, and was said to have dedicated his throne to the shrine at Delphi. There were many stories about the wealth of Croesus. Croesus was said to have offered royal gifts not only to the shrine at Delphi, but to Apollo's shrine at Didyma, near Miletus, as well. Relations between the Lydians and the Greeks in Asia Minor were not always friendly, of course. Herodotus speaks on more than one occasion of soldiers sent against Ionian towns by the rulers of Lydia. He also recorded (1, 94) that 'as far as we know, the Lydians were the first to use coins of gold and silver, and the first people to live by trading.'

It can be assumed from numismatic material found in the cities of Asia Minor, and particularly in the temple of Artemis at Ephesus, that by the end of the seventh century the Ionians and the Lydians were minting metal coins. They were pieces of electrum, of specified weight; this natural alloy of gold and silver was mined in Lydia. One side of the coin was impressed with a design, usually square in shape (*quadratum incusum*), while on the other side was the symbol of the state which issued the coin and at the same time guaranteed its value. Lydian coins bear either a lion's head or a lion's paw. At first these coins may have been minted to pay the wages of mercenaries in the service of Lydia, among whom there were many Greeks of Asia Minor.

Excavation of the royal palaces at Pasargadae and Persepolis has revealed that there were Greek craftsmen and artists working for Cyrus, who had defeated Croesus and founded the Persian Empire, and for his successors. This does not of course mean that relations between the Greeks of Asia Minor and those in power in Persia were friendly. According to Herodotus (1, 141) Cyrus blamed the Greeks for not taking his side against Croesus in the war against Lydia. The Milesians were the only Greeks with whom Cyrus made a pact on the same terms as they had enjoyed under the Lydian king. The people of two of the Greek cities found the new situation intolerable and preferred to emigrate. The Phocaeans, as we have seen, moved first to Alalia in Corsica and then on to Hyele (Elea) in southern Italy. Some of the citizens of Teos moved to the northern shores of the Aegean and settled in Abdera, while others penetrated to the northern coast of the Black Sea and founded a colony called Phanagoria, on the Cimmerian Bosphorus (now the Straits of Kerch).

With the rise of the great Persian Empire political conditions in the eastern Mediterranean changed, and the Greek cities of Asia Minor lost their privileged position in trade and navigation. Not long after he had defeated Lydia, Cyrus conquered Babylonia and Syria; the Persians could then make use of the Phoenician fleet to guard their interests on the western fringes of the empire. Trade between the Greeks of Asia Minor and the Egyptians lost its importance when Egypt became part of the Persian Empire, under Cambyses (525). When Darius ruled the Empire the Persians were masters of the Hellespont, thus controlling access to an area where there were many Greek colonies, mainly founded by Ionian cities. The Greeks of Asia Minor also found it hard to accept Persian restriction of their political autonomy, when the satrap of Sardes put his followers into their cities to rule as tyrants. Tension reached its height in the year 500 or 499 BC, and the Greeks of Asia Minor rose against the Persians, thus opening the first phase of the Persian Wars. This marked not only a new chapter in the history of Graeco-Persian relations, but a new epoch in Greek history.

The Greeks of Asia Minor, as we have already seen, played an important part in contacts between Egypt and Greece. Egyptian influences soon appeared in Greek art alongside those of the Near Eastern cultures, probably carried at first by Phoenician and Syrian contacts. Egyptian imports are first attested from Crete and Samos, and it was a citizen of Samos, Kolaios, who is said to have been driven to the Atlantic coast of Spain when he set out for Egypt. It was at this time, in the second half of the seventh century, that conditions in Egypt became more settled; Psammetichus (Psamtek) I, founder of the dynasty of Saïs, strengthened his hold on the land with the help of Ionian and Carian mercenaries, according to Herodotus (2, 152). The soldiers apparently set sail 'for booty' and were driven from their course on to the shores of Egypt. Here they took service with the king, and were rewarded by Psammetichus with land to settle on. Thus units of Greeks and Carians from Asia Minor became part of the army of the dynasty of Saïs, in which other mercenaries came from Nubia and Libya, Syria, Phoenicia and Palestine. The Jewish soldiers were stationed in southern Egypt, on the island of Elephantine near Assuan. Authentic evidence of the presence of Greek mercenaries has survived at Abu Simbel, even further south, near the present Egyptian-Sudanese border. Greek soldiers taking part in the campaign of Psammetichus II against Nubia carved an inscription on the left foot of the colossus of Rameses II, at the beginning of the sixth century.

Besides Greek soldiers, there were Greek traders who settled in Egypt. According to Herodotus (2, 178), King Ahmose who ruled Egypt from the early sixties of the sixth century allowed them to settle in Naucratis, in the Nile delta, not far from Saïs, the centre of the Egyptian kingdom at that time. Naucratis was not an agricultural colony, but a trading centre like the earlier one at Al-Mina in Syria. Traders from many Greek states lived there, and according to Herodotus those from Miletus set up a temple to Apollo, those from Samos a temple to Hera, and those from Aegina a temple dedicated to Zeus. Besides these temples a sacred precinct had been built, called the Hellenion, to which many of the cities of Asia Minor had contributed.

Most of these buildings have been excavated by archaeologists working at Naucratis, and it has also been proved that Greeks began to settle there several decades before Amasis (Ahmose) came to the throne, at the latest in the last quarter of the seventh century. Among the pottery found, imports from Asia Minor predominate, together with that of neighbouring islands, while goods from Corinth, Sparta and Athens are also present. There were Greek craftsmen working in Naucratis, too; scarab-shaped seals were made there, of material resembling the faience of Renaissance Italy. Wine and olive oil were imported into Egypt through Naucratis, while the chief exports were grains, and perhaps papyrus and linen.

There were Greek settlements elsewhere in Egypt, too. The city of Daphnae (now Tell Defenneh) in the eastern part of the delta was built during the reign of Psammetichus I, as a fortress protecting Egypt from the danger of attacks launched from Arabia and Syria. Jews and Greeks predominated among the inhabitants. Sixth-century Greek pottery has also been found in ancient Egyptian centres like Memphis and Thebes (Veset), and on some other sites. When the Persians conquered Egypt, the Greeks settled there suffered too, and it is not until the turn of the sixth century BC that Greek imports again came to Naucratis, mostly Athenian pottery and coins.

Unlike Naucratis in Egypt, Cyrene in Libya was agricultural in character. In the sixth century this colony founded by Thera was so prosperous that new settlers were lured there from the Peloponnese and from the Dorian islands in the Aegean Sea. More new colonies were thus founded in Libya. When Egypt lost her independence all the Greek colonies in Libya found themselves subject to her Persian rulers.

Colonization in the Aegean region was first directed towards the north-west coast, where settlers from Eretria and Chalcis came from Euboea. In the north the Greeks were met by an armed and hostile Thracian population. These conflicts are reflected in the verse of one of the earliest Greek lyric poets, Archilochus of Paros, who was engaged in the fighting between the Thracian inhabitants of the island of Thasos and the neighbouring mainland coast and the Parians, about the middle of the seventh century. There was a colony founded from Paros on the island of Thasos as early as c.680 BC. The settlers did not have an easy time there. Archilochus complained that he had to be constantly on the alert, kneading his bread with his spear and pressing his wine in similar fashion, and even when he drank it, he did so leaning on his spear. In another poem he admitted to losing his shield 'somewhere in the bushes' while fighting Thracian warriors. Elsewhere, in lines cursing a friend for betraying him, Archilochus depicts the dangerous life of Greek sailors coasting off the shores of Thrace. He wishes his friend the worst fate — may the waves bear him all the way to Salmydessus (a point on the Black Sea coast west of the Bosphorus, where there was a Thracian settlement of that name) and may the Thracians give him a proper welcome and force him to eat the 'bread of slavery'.

That the Greeks settling the northern shores of the Aegean met with resistance from the local inhabitants is also borne out by the fate of the settlers from Clazomenae who were forced to leave their colony at Abdera under persistent Thracian attacks. It was not until the middle of the sixth century that Abdera was again colonized, this time by citizens of Teos who emigrated, as we have already seen, because they did not want to live under Persian rule. There was plenty of timber for building in Thrace, and the Greek colonies founded there soon became famous for their vineyards. It was mainly citizens of Miletus and Megara who settled there, the latter founding Chalcedon (now Kadiköy) on the Asian coast at the entrance to the Bosphorus, and later Byzantium (the Istanbul of today) on a very fine site on the European side. Classical authors traditionally dated Megarian colonization of the Black Sea straits as early as the end of the eighth century, and the founding of Byzantium in 660 BC, but the archaeological evidence would support a later date.

The colony of Sigeum lay on the Asian side of the entrance to the Hellespont, and was the cause of fierce fighting between Mytilene and Athens at the end of the seventh century, the conflict being settled, it was said, by the tyrant of Corinth, Periander. The Athenians were given the settlement of Sigeum but Mytilene got the fortress controlling access to the coast. The Athenians do not seem to have had complete control of Sigeum until the time of the tyrant Peisistratus. There is an illustration of Athenian influence in the colony on the tombstone of one Phanodicus of Proconnesus, who lived in Sigeum and was buried there; the inscription, in both the Ionian and the Attic dialects, dates from the middle or perhaps the beginning of the sixth century.

Mytilene acquired a strong position in Thracian Chersonese, while Miletus dominated the Black Sea region, their very first settlement there, Sinope on the southern coast, dating from as early as 800 BC, according to Greek tradition. In the middle of the eighth century Sinope was said to have founded Trapezus, but there was already a tradition in classical antiquity that Sinope was founded anew in the middle or later seventh century. The Greeks clearly penetrated into the Black Sea area very early, as we can see from the legends of the Argonauts, Medea, and the time spent by Iphigenia, Agamemnon's daughter, among the Tauri. Hesiod had already written of the River Phasis in Colchis (now the Rion). Colonies do not seem to have arisen on the Black Sea coast before those founded in the straits, however. Miletus founded Amisus between Sinope and Trapezus. The most westerly colony on the southern Black Sea coast was

Heracleia, called Pontica (after the Black Sea region) to distinguish it from other colonies of that name. It was founded about the middle of the sixth century by settlers from Megara and from Tanagra in Boeotia.

The earliest Greek settlement on the western coast of the Black Sea was furthest from the Straits of the Bosphorus, on a site south of the delta of the greatest of European rivers. The lower reaches of the Danube were called Istros in ancient times, and the name was taken by this colony founded from Miletus (Istros, Histria, Istropolis). The so-called Pseudo-Skymnos, Hellenistic author of a tale in verse about sailing the Black Sea, said that Istros was founded at the end of the seventh century, and excavation has provided archaeological confirmation for the date. The earliest material remains even suggest that Greek settlement here may have been as early as the middle of the seventh century, which agrees with another classical tradition recorded by the early Christian chronicler, Eusebius. That the colony carried on trade with the local inhabitants is proved by finds of Greek archaic pottery on Thracian sites in the vicinity.

Round about 600 BC Apollonia (now Sozopol) was founded in the southern part of the western Black Sea, and during the first half of the sixth century two more followed, on the sites of what are now two of the largest ports in the western Black Sea, Odessus (now Varna) and Tomi or Tomis (now Constanza). Here too Megara came into conflict with Miletus, founder of all these colonies.

In the northern Black Sea region Greek pottery of the last quarter of the seventh century is attested on the island of Berezan, at the joint mouth of the Dnieper and the Bug. The population here was Scythian, and Greek settlement seems to have remained a trading-post (*emporion*). A permanent Greek colony was later set up on the right bank of the Bug and called Olbia ('The Fortunate'). Later colonies were also founded on sites with good communications inland: Tyras in the west, at the mouth of the river of the same name (now the Dniester), and Panticapaeum to the east on the Cimmerian Bosphorus.

Archaeological investigation suggests that the Greeks settled

Panticapaeum from the end of the seventh century onwards, and that their relations with the local inhabitants were close. Some later left Panticapaeum to found other colonies. Theodosia on the southern coast of the Taurian Chersonese was founded from Miletus, probably in the first half of the sixth century. Two more Milesian colonies, Phasis and Dioscurias, lay on the eastern shores of the Black Sea, and were linked with the legend of the Argonauts by Greek tradition. It is difficult to determine when they were settled, but local coins minted at the beginning of the fifth century have been found in Phasis, and it is probable that the colony arose at the end of the archaic period.

The Black Sea became a lively part of the Greek world, as can be seen from the names the Greeks gave it. The sailors who navigated the stormy Black Sea waters and found the local people distrustful of them, interpreted the Old Persian name *achšaena* (black) as *axeinos* ('inhospitable'). It was not until they came to know the Black Sea coast better and to settle there, that they began to call it 'hospitable', Pontos Euxeinos. Herodotus (4, 53) described the lower reaches of the Dnieper as a region of good pastures, with soil that was fertile for grain growing, and with 'large tuna-fish without bones, called *antakaioi* ('sturgeons'), which are salted down'. Excavations at Tyritaca (a settlement south of Panticapaeum) did in fact reveal tanks for salting fish, with remains of bones and scales. As well as exporting dried and salted fish, the Black Sea became a valuable source of grain supplies; Scythian and Thracian slaves were also brought to Greece from colonies in the Black Sea area.

The colonization of the northern Black Sea region brought the Greeks into contact not only with the people living along the coast, but with those from much further inland. As well as the Tauri, Cimmerians and Sauromatae (Sarmatians), Herodotus speaks of many other tribes and peoples we cannot identify with certainty.

The fact that Greek colonies stretched from the western shores of the Mediterranean right to Colchis on the Black Sea meant that the horizons of the Greek world were broad indeed, and contributed no little to the economic and cultural evolution of that world. It did not take place without considerable conflict however, not only between the pioneers and the local people of the regions they settled in, but also between the founding Greek cities themselves, especially the most active ones. One such conflict was that between Chalcis and Eretria over the fertile plain in the valley of the Lelantus (now the Kalamontari) which lay between the two Euboean cities. Beginning probably at the end of the eighth century, this local conflict over contested territory grew into a long war in which, according to Thucydides (1, 15), 'the other Greeks' also took part, on both sides. Herodotus gives more detailed information when, in connection with the help later given by Eretria to the Ionians of Asia Minor (who, headed by Miletus, rose against the Persians in the early fifth century), he records that Eretria was only paying back an old debt (5, 99). This is a reference to the fact that the Milesians took the side of Eretria, while Samos supported Chalcis, in the earlier conflict. From other sources it appears that Corinth also came in on the side of Chalcis, while Chios and perhaps Megara as well supported Eretria.

Some scholars have even gone so far as to put forward a theory of two 'mercantile alliances', mutually hostile, in archaic Greece, competing for control over the sources of raw materials and over markets for their products. This approach is exaggerated in its over-estimation of the mercantile nature of Greek civilization and its view of the ancient world as through modern eyes. It is of course clear that the Lelantine war had its effect on the process of colonization. The friendly co-operation between Chalcis and Eretria when they founded settlements in southern Italy and on Chalcidice turned to enmity, and there was hostility between other cities, too.

We have a unique source of knowledge for the time, which gives a detailed description of the life of the Boeotian peasants, Hesiod's poem *Works and Days*. Unlike Homer, who remains hidden behind the vast stream of events before Troy, on Ithaca and elsewhere, Hesiod was an absolutely authentic historical person. He himself tells us that his father came from Aeolian Cyme and was engaged in overseas trade. He was not lucky, however, and moved from Asia Minor to Boeotia, settling 'in the poor village of Ascra not far from

Helicon', where 'winter is bad, summer difficult, and it is never pleasant.' Hesiod himself only saw the sea when he went to Chalcis to take part in a poetic contest and had to cross the straits of Euripus separating Boeotia from the island of Euboea. Nevertheless he gives good advice to those who want to sail the seas, on the time of year to choose. At the same time he warns against bold ventures undertaken only to acquire riches, and stresses the dangers of entrusting one's whole wealth to ships which easily fall prey to the wild waves.

Hesiod believed that the best way to earn a living was from the soil. The farm he describes from his own experience is not a large one, and is worked by the peasant with his wife and a few helpers, among whom there are slaves (*dmoes*), a labourer with no home of his own (*thes aoikos*), and a farm servant (*erithos*) who is also not supposed to have a family of her own, in order to devote herself entirely to her duties on the master's farm. In spite of the everlasting hard work Hesiod describes in such detail, the peasant may be ruined by bad weather or some other catastrophe, and then he can only beg a loan from some more fortunate neighbour. He himself is also bound to help others in difficulty. The best thing is to have but one son, who then inherits the whole farm (*oikos*) from his father. To have the property broken up among a number of heirs was of course unfavourable, and this was the reason younger sons often left their native city to find land and a living elsewhere. Hesiod had a personal reason for this discussion of the question of inheritance; as he says in the introduction to his poem, and again later, he had cause to reproach his brother Perses for his behaviour. When the family property was divided between the two brothers at their father's death, Hesiod was badly cheated by his brother.

The daily struggle with the elements and his personal misfortunes undoubtedly contributed to Hesiod's pessimistic view of the world. He recounts the legend of Pandora's box, inside which Zeus sent trouble and sickness into the world to punish man, because Prometheus had brought them fire against his prohibition. Hesiod's attitude is even more clearly expressed in the myth of the five generations of man. The ideal golden age under the rule of Kronos, when

115

men 'lived like gods', was followed by the silver age, the bronze age, the age of heroes, and finally the present iron age.

Hesiod took a grim view of the future, prophesying the breakdown of the family and of human relationships altogether; right would give way to might and *Aidos* ('sense of shame') and *Nemesis* ('righteous anger') would be lost from the world. The poet had his reasons for this gloomy view; during the hearing of the case of their inheritance, his brother Perses had cunningly found favour with the 'kings anxious for gifts' (*basileis dorophagoi*, literally, 'kings devouring gifts') and thus they gave the decision in his favour. Hesiod utters critical judgment on venial aristocrats and warns them that Zeus will punish them if they knowingly deform the law and give false judgment. His poem is a hymn of praise to conscientious and well-thought-out work, to man in harmony with his land, and also a passionate plea for order and right (*dike*) and an indictment of arbitrary and arrogant power. The road to evil is smooth and level, but the path of righteousness (*arete*) must be watered with man's sweat.

Conflict between the aristocrats and the ordinary people was even more marked in those cities which were in the forefront of the economic development of archaic Greece. At the time of the migrations which followed the fall of the Mycenaean civilization, and after the arrival of the Dorian and north-western tribes on the Greek mainland, the tribal organization of society was strengthened. Chieftains, kings (basileis) stood at the head of the tribes (phylae), concentrating both military and civil executive power in their hands. Greek tradition preserved the memory of a time when the privileged position of the kings was held within certain bounds in many cities. Already in the early phase of the archaic period the royal function had been taken over by leaders who were called prytans (*prytanis*, 'superior,' 'chairman') or archons (*archon*, 'leader,' 'ruler'), who were taken solely from the ranks of the aristocracy and in some cities only from certain families. Like the kings, the aristocrats based their power on the tribal system, and it is natural that tradition marks no sharp break between the time of royal and aristocratic rule.

Although the aristocrats formed a privileged social group and concentrated both the executive power and economic privilege in their own hands (particularly as regards land tenure), as individuals they ruled only for a certain specified period. Men of lower social standing began to push themselves forward, particularly those who had contributed to the prosperity of the community: merchants and craftsmen. In some places even the peasants began to show their resentment of the privileges enjoyed by the aristocratic families. Matters were made worse by conflicts between the different groups of aristocratic families, and it was no wonder that ambitious individuals — usually aristocrats — seized the opportunity to take power by force. The Greeks called these autocrats 'tyrants'.

The term *tyrannos* probably comes originally from Asia Minor. In the early Greek cities the rule of a tyrant was a frequent phenomenon; he usually seized power from an aristocratic government by force of arms, and, although his prime motive was personal ambition, as a rule the tyrant advanced the prosperity of the community and ensured social stability. 'Tyranny' thus represented a significant stage in the evolution of the city-state (polis).

The sources allow us to trace the history of certain states in the archaic period, at least in outline, and particularly the history of Corinth. After the power of the kings had been broken, the city was ruled by the Bacchiads during the second half of the eighth and the first half of the seventh century; this was a family claiming descent from one of the kings of Corinth. Classical writers describe the arrogance of the Bacchiads, and accuse them of appropriating the profits of the city's trade. Unrest broke out in a rising led by Cypselus, whose mother came of the Bacchiad family but whose father was of pre-Dorian origin, perhaps Achaean. Cypselus used his position as military commander to settle accounts with the Bacchiads, killing some and forcing others to flee. Their property was confiscated and divided among the supporters of Cypselus, and especially among the peasants who served under his command as hoplites.

The tyranny of Cypselus lasted for thirty years, and was followed

117

(probably in the twenties of the seventh century) by that of his son Periander, given a place in later Greek tradition among the Seven Sages. Periander continued the anti-aristocratic policy of his father, built up a fleet and is even said to have proposed cutting a channel through the isthmus of Corinth. This project was of course far beyond the technical possibilities of the day, but archaeological investigation has revealed the remains of *diolkos*, by means of which ships were towed overland from one Corinthian port to another; Lechaion lay in the Gulf of Corinth and maintained contact with the region round the Ionian Sea, Sicily and southern Italy, while Kenchreai on the Saronic Gulf was the gateway to the Aegean. Further evidence of the economic prosperity of Corinth were the coins minted with a winged Pegasus, the symbol of the city, on the face.

Towards the end of his reign, which lasted over forty years, Periander was forced to deal with growing opposition to the system of personal power he represented. He formed an armed bodyguard of three hundred men. His nephew Psammetichus succeeded him, named after the Egyptian king of the Saïte dynasty, with whom the Cypselus family seems to have been on friendly terms. Psammetichus only ruled for three years before tyrannic rule was abolished in Corinth, probably in the late eighties of the sixth century. There was no return to aristocratic rule, but a new regime was installed, based on the territorial distribution of all Corinthian citizens, regardless of origin, in eight phylae.

Tyrants remained longest in power in Sicyon. Here the tyranny was set up by Orthagoras, who belonged to the pre-Dorian section of the population, and like Cypselus in Corinth, made use of his position as military commander to seize power. He seems to have been succeeded by his brother Myron, victor in the Olympic Games of 648 BC. The most famous of the tyrants of Sicyon was the grandson of Myron, Cleisthenes, but his genealogy is not entirely reliable.

Cleisthenes had great success in the First Sacred War, at the beginning of the sixth century, when the Greek cities fought the people of Krisa in Phocis, who abused their proximity to the Delphic shrine to attack pilgrims on their way to worship Apollo. Later on Cleisthenes fought against Argos, and made use of this opportunity to introduce a number of measures against the Dorians in Sicyon. The most significant of these was the renaming of the phylae; the pre-Dorian phyle to which he himself belonged was given the name *Archelaoi* ('rulers of the people'), while the three Dorian phylae (Hylleis, Dymanes and Pamphyloi) received derisive names. The fame of this tyrant of Sicyon is shown in the story Herodotus tells of the marriage of his daughter Agariste; twelve suitors from different parts of the Greek world sought her hand, but it was an Athenian, Megacles of the family of the Alcmeonids, who became Cleisthenes' son-in-law. The tyranny of the Orthagorids ended not long after the death of Cleisthenes, but the names he gave to the phylae persisted until the turn of the sixth century, when Sicyon became a member of the Peloponnesian League.

In the second half of the seventh century Megara was also ruled by a tyrant, Theagenes, who overthrew the aristocrats with the help of his armed followers. Little is known of his rule, and we do not even know how long it lasted. The only chronological guide to his reign is the record that his son-in-law, the Athenian Cylon, was a victor in the Olympic Games of 640 BC, and later tried to become tyrant of Athens.

According to Plutarch (*Moral.* 295 CD) a 'reasonable government' was set up in Megara after Theagenes had been overthrown, but social conflict broke out again with renewed force early on. Conditions in Megara in the sixth century are illustrated in the verse of the Megarian poet Theognis, who criticized the social changes which were taking place, speaking from the conservative standpoint and defending the old order in which the aristocracy set the tone. Megara suffered a heavy defeat at the hands of the Athenians, losing the island of Salamis and then the port of Nisaea. After the middle of the sixth century Megara no longer held her earlier position of importance in overseas trade.

We have also considerable records of social conflict in the Greek cities in Asia Minor. At the end of the seventh century Thrasybulus became tyrant of Miletus, and it was under him that the attacks of the Lydian King Alyattes were successfully driven off. Coins minted with the symbol of a lion testify to the economic prosperity the city enjoyed. Thrasybulus maintained friendly relations with Periander, and is said to have advised the latter to be uncompromising in dealing with the Corinthian opposition to his rule. The names of other tyrants in Miletus are also known, and the record has come down to us of fighting between rich and poor there, which only ceased after the citizens of the island of Paros intervened to make peace. Towards the end of the archaic period Miletus, like the other Greek cities in Asia Minor, came under Persian rule, and the tyrant Histiaeus who was in power at the time ruled only by leave of the Persian king.

In Ephesus Pythagoras overthrew the aristocrats around the year 600 BC. He is described by the writers of antiquity as a cruel tyrant who confiscated the property of his political opponents and distributed some of it among the people. It was probably during his reign that Ephesus began to mint coins bearing the symbol of a bee. The names of other tyrants of Ephesus are known, but there is nothing from which to reconstruct the history of the city during the archaic period.

We have better knowledge of the early history of Mytilene on the island of Lesbos. The ruling aristocrats from the Penthelid house were overthrown by Melanchros, but he did not remain in power for long. Tyranny was renewed here later by Myrsilus, who also took strong measures against the aristocracy. The struggle is echoed in the verse of Alcaeus, who describes Mytilene in one poem as a boat tossed on the stormy waves, and elsewhere rejoices at the death of the hated tyrant. The aristocrats, who hoped for help from abroad, were disappointed, however; the people of Mytilene entrusted the city to Pittacus, electing him their *aesymnetes* ('arbitrator', 'ruler'). Alcaeus vents his wrath on him, but Pittacus was liked and respected in Mytilene; he earned military honours in the war against Athens over Sigeum, and when, ten years after he was installed, the stability and prosperity of the city were assured, he voluntarily relinquished office.

One of the most famous tyrants in archaic Greece was Polycrates of Samos, who came to power about the year 540 BC. Under his rule Samos became the most powerful state in the Aegean region. He had a large fleet, expanded the port of Samos, installed a water supply and undertook other civil engineering projects. He invited craftsmen, artists and poets to Samos, two of the finest being Ibycus of Rhegium and Anacreon of Teos. The tyrant of Samos maintained friendly relations with King Amasis (Ahmose) of Egypt, but when Cambyses, king of Persia, set out to attack Egypt, Polycrates sent his ships to assist the Persians. In spite of this, the Persians did not like the idea of a strong Greek state so close to the mainland of Asia Minor, and had Polycrates assassinated. Samos then came under Persian rule.

Social conflict broke out in many Greek cities during the seventh and sixth centuries, and records of tyrants who overthrew aristocratic regimes exist for the early history of Colophon, Erythrae, Chios, Lindos on Rhodes, and Naxos. In later accounts the tyrant of Lindos, Cleobulus, was given a place among the Seven Sages. Lygdamis of Naxos is known to have been on friendly terms with the Athenian tyrant Peisistratus and with Polycrates of Samos. In the sixth century there were tyrants for a short time in the Euboean cities of Chalcis and Eretria.

The situation differed somewhat in the Greek colonies in Sicily and southern Italy, where family ties were not as important as in the home cities of Greece. The colonists had to deal with the local inhabitants and also with Etruscan and especially with Carthaginian competition. They had to be in a permanent state of military alert, which provided excellent opportunity for ambitious leaders to seize power for themselves. The names of several tyrants who ruled in the Sicilian and southern Italian cities in the archaic period have come down to us, one of the most famous being Phalaris who reigned in Acragas in the second quarter of the sixth century. He fought against the Sicans and tried to extend his influence to neighbouring Greek settlements. Tyranny did not reach major proportions in Sicily until the first half of the fifth century, however.

It is thus possible to trace marked social changes in the city-states which led the way to economic and cultural growth in archaic Greece, in the course of the seventh and sixth centuries BC. There were various local factors which influenced the course of events, but the general tendency was to move away from tribal forms of society, in which aristocratic families played the decisive role, towards the formation of the city-state (polis) based on a constitution and accepting legal norms. We have most information about this evolution from the history of Athens.

CHAPTER V

Political and Social History
of Athens

A certain degree of continuity with the Mycenaean civilization persisted in Attica, and it was here that the Protogeometric style evolved in pottery, with vessels shaped like those of the sub-Mycenaean style. In the early ninth century the Geometric style developed in Attica, as well as in the Argolis and somewhat later in Corinth and Boeotia, and lasted for about two hundred years. New elements in the decoration began to appear about 800 BC, as Athenian craftsmen absorbed impulses from the east, incorporating plant motifs in geometrical composition, and then moved on to stylized human figures. In the second half of the eighth century production of pottery increased rapidly, but Attic pottery gradually lost its dominating position in the Greek world and that of Corinth began to take its place in Greek exports.

Literary references to the early phase of Athenian history, like the record of the early history of other Greek cities, belong to the world of myth, but nevertheless they reflect the general trend of evolution towards political organization of the people living in Attica. According to the account recorded by Aristotle in his *Athenian Constitution* (41, 2), 'the first change in the original conditions' is said to have taken place 'when Ion and his companions settled there together. It was then that the people were divided for the first time into four phylae and leaders of each phyle established (the *phylobasileis*).' This division into four phylae (Geleontes, Hopletes, Argadeis and Aigikoreis) was common to all the Ionians, although as we saw in Chapter II other names are found among the Ionians of Asia Minor. They were probably adopted after the Ionians settled in their new home. It can be assumed that this traditional grouping of four phylae was already established before the Ionians migrated to the Aegean islands and the western coast of Asia Minor.

Aristotle links the next stage in the evolution of Athenian society with the name of Theseus, to whom Greek tradition ascribed the synoecism (*synoikismos*, 'moving together'), that is to say the unification of Attica in a single community with its centre in Athens. We read in Thucydides (2, 15) that Theseus 'abolished the councils and offices in the other cities and moved them all to the present city, where he set up a single council chamber and *prytaneion*'. Plutarch gives the same information in his *Life of Theseus* (24) and adds (25) that Theseus divided the people of Athens into three groups: '*eupatrids, geomori*, and *demiurgi*'.

This is of course a fiction, enabling later writers to link the presumed early phase of Athenian history with the greatest hero of Athenian antiquity. Indeed, in his introduction to what he has to say about Theseus, Plutarch comments that events at the beginning of the history of Athens 'are neither trustworthy nor certain' and begs his readers to accept his story 'with kind indulgence'. In Athenian myth Theseus is credited with heroic feats like those attributed to the Mycenaean heroes Perseus and Heracles. In one of the best-known legends Theseus liberates his country from humiliating subjection to the rulers of Crete. The story of the labyrinth of Knossos, the Minotaur and Ariadne all belong to the Minoan-Mycenaean myths.

The changes in society attributed to Theseus were undoubtedly much later than the traditions of antiquity suggest. Assuming that the division into four Ionian phylae took place in Attica after the decline of Mycenaean civilization and before the Ionian migration to Asia Minor, synoecism must have occurred late in the 'Dark Ages', at the beginning of the archaic period. It was of course a slow process, the last phase culminating in the inclusion of Eleusis in the south-west, probably in the seventh century.

In Attica, as in other parts of Greece, phratries are attested as part of the tribal system. A law which has survived incomplete in a late fifth century inscription from Athens, and is also mentioned by Demosthenes (43, 57), deals with the punishment of those who have committed manslaughter. If the victim had no close relatives, his interests were to be furthered by ten members of his phratry, chosen 'for their birth' (*aristinden*). Solon's law on autonomy for organizations allowed phratries and other groups of citizens the right to make decisions, provided they did not run counter to the law of the polis. Among the groups of citizens named here we find *gennetai* ('members of the clans', *gene*) and *orgeones*. From a fragment of a chronicle of Athens written about 300 BC by Philochorus, we learn that members of a phratry accepted into their midst both members of the clans and orgeones.

The difference between these two groups of Athenian citizens is not clear. The clan (*genos*) is usually taken to be the smallest unit of the tribal organization, and thus part of the phratry. In archaic Athens it appears to have been the aristocrats who were grouped in the clans, and enjoyed (as in other states) certain privileges. The orgeones would then be the free men of Attica who were not members of the clans. They may have been excluded from the clans when the aristocrats took them over. Other writers believe that the orgeones were not in the clans because they were the descendants of immigrants. Other scholars again suggest that they were the descendants of the ancient pre-Ionian inhabitants of Attica.

The information at our disposal does not allow us to form a reliable picture of the social structure of each element in the tribal system in Attica. I consider nevertheless that there is no justification for the view that the phratries — or even the phylae — originally included only aristocrats. If the members of the phratry who were to attain justice for a victimized fellow were chosen 'for their birth', it suggests that there were not only aristocrats in the phratry. We can also quote in this connection the statement in a fragment of Aristotle (385, edited by V. Rose) that the Athenians had been divided into four phylae at one time, each phyle being composed of three phratries and each phratry of thirty clans of thirty men. This is of course a later construction reflecting the influence of the calendar (4 seasons, 12 months and 360 days). Nevertheless it is obvious that Aristotle could not have thought that there were almost 11,000 aristocratic families in Attica; he clearly meant the tribal organization (including phratries and gene) to apply to the whole of the population.

If synoecism was the outcome of a long evolution, it is even more likely to be the case for the division of the people of Attica into three groups, which was also ascribed to Theseus. As described earlier, Plutarch puts the eupatrids first, before the peasants (geomori) and the craftsmen (demiurgi). The name for the first group, which could also be translated as 'the sons of good (noble) fathers', was used for the aristocrats of Athens by other classical authors, too. In Athens, as in other states, the power of the kings had been abolished and their place taken by officials chosen from the aristocratic families. They were called *archontes* ('rulers') and were at first elected for life, later for a period of ten years, and from the first half of the seventh century they held office only for one year. Aristotle had already noted this gradual shortening of their period of office, in his *Athenian Constitution* (3, 1). This particular version, however, seems to have arisen as a result of the efforts of the local chroniclers of Athens (atthidographoi) to explain the gap between the rule of the mythical kings and the period of rule by the archons, the list of whose names only went back to the year 682/1 BC.

In Athens the year was given the name (*onoma, onyma*) of the supreme archon, who thus came to be known as the *archon eponymos*. In addition to the supreme archon, who wielded executive and judiciary power, an *archon polemarchos* was elected every year to lead the army, and an *archon basileus* whose office covered matters of religion. Later they were assisted by six officials known as *thesmothetai* ('law-givers'), who saw to it that the laws were respected. Aristotle stressed at two points in the relevant chapter of his *Athenian*

126

Constitution (3,1 and 3,6) that the archons were chosen 'for their birth and their wealth'. Former archons became members of the council which met on a hill (*pagos*) below the Acropolis which was dedicated to Ares, and given the name (the council on) the Areopagus.

The eupatrids combined their political power with their position in the economic life of Athens, based mainly on their ownership of the land. Agriculture was the principal form of production in all the city-states of ancient Greece. In Athens, with her vast agricultural hinterland, the peasant question was particularly important. Although we can hardly take literally Aristotle's comment that 'all the land was in the hands of a few men (*di'oligon*)' (*Ath.Const.* 2,2), it is clear that there was great inequality in the ownership of land.

At the very bottom of the scale there were those peasants who had become subject to the eupatrids and were called *hektemorioi* or *hektemoroi* ('sixth-part men'). Even among classical writers views differed as to whether the hektemorioi gave one sixth of their crops to the eupatrids, or whether they were allowed to keep only one sixth of the whole harvest. Aristotle in his *Athenian Constitution* (2,2) used the term *misthosis* ('rent') for this sixth of the harvest, which would favour the former interpretation. Plutarch (*Life of Solon* 13) also recorded that the hektemorioi delivered up 'one sixth of the harvest' to the rich. Later authors, on the other hand, mostly assert that the peasants had to subsist on one sixth of their harvest. Both these interpretations are based on an etymological explanation of a term which is itself unclear. Nor are modern scholars agreed on the point; some have suggested that one sixth of the yield from the fields they cultivated could not have given the peasants a living, while others have pointed out that to deliver one sixth of the harvest would not have been such a dire burden as Aristotle and other writers of antiquity depict. It is clear that the real amount delivered depended on the size and fertility of the land concerned, so that there could have been considerable differences between the positions in which individual peasants found themselves. It seems reasonable, therefore, to seek another interpretation. The basic measure of volume, the *medimnos*, was divided into six parts, each sixth being a *hekteus*. It is possible that the quotas to be delivered by the hektemorioi were calculated in sixths of a medimnos, while the number of hekteis per medimnos to be delivered could be set variously. Another interpretation which has been put forward suggests that the hektemorioi pledged themselves to work off their quota on the master's land in six instalments, usually in six consecutive years. In fact these hypotheses are all, like those of the ancient writers, based on the interpretation given to the term hektemorioi.

The earliest testimony to the life of the peasants dependent on rich masters is presented by an author who not only lived in archaic Athens himself, but also made a significant contribution to the solution of social problems in his native state. In lines quoted by Aristotle in his *Athenian Constitution* and also partially by Plutarch in his *Life of Solon*, this great poet, philosopher and statesman of Athens declared — although he did not specifically mention the hektemorioi — that 'he had cleared from the dark earth the landmarks that still stood firmly in many places. From slavery it passed to freedom' (fragment 24; ed. E. Diehl). We cannot doubt that these landmarks (*horoi*) marked the fields worked by peasants subject to their masters, but even with this, the earliest evidence we have, it is impossible to deduce anything of the character of that subjection, or how it evolved.

The basic problem is that we know nothing about the nature of land ownership in archaic Athens. Earlier scholars were predominantly of the opinion that there was unlimited private ownership of land. Situations familiar from classical Greece and even legal concepts current in Roman law were then applied to conditions obtaining before the time of Solon. Some writers tried to find an analogy for the hektemorioi in the Roman client relationship, and assumed that the peasants voluntarily accepted the authority of the rich landowners in order to protect themselves from being sold into slavery for debt. It is now clear, however, that in Athens at that time individual owners could not dispose of their land as they liked, but that at least part of it, the original lot granted to them, remained the inalienable property of the family. It is extremely unlikely that there existed anything so involved as a fictive sale of land with the possibility of repurchase, as some have suggested. If it is true that the peasant was not free to dispose of his land as he wished, then he must have been obliged to give his creditors a guarantee not by pledging his property, but by binding his own person or those of members of his family. If he then failed to meet his obligations, he or his children would be sold as slaves.

Social antagonisms increased as the population grew, a factor which can be observed in other Greek city-states at the same period. In Attica, in addition, changes took place in the nature of the cultivation of the land, and this, too, had a social impact. The eupatrids planted vineyards and olive groves, and thus drew greater profit from their land than the small peasants, who had to use every corner of theirs for grain, in order to provide a living for their families, and could not invest in crops which would not give any return for several years.

The crafts had a long tradition in Attica, particularly pottery. At the turn of the eighth century Geometric pottery was replaced by a new style which introduced oriental elements into the decoration, known as Proto-Attic pottery. At first it is found only in the immediate vicinity of Attica, but it later spread to all parts of the Greek world. In the last quarter of the seventh century the Proto-Attic style merged into that of the black figure vases, which marked the peak of Greek pottery and vase painting. Black figure ware was soon attested from Naucratis, Etruria and Massalia. In the course of the sixth century Attic black figure ware pushed the pottery of Corinth and Asia Minor into the background, and thus the Athenians acquired an ever more important place in craft production and trade throughout the Mediterranean.

In the second half of the seventh century Athens was already torn by the same social conflicts that were developing in other Greek states. The Athenian aristocrat Cylon, as recounted in the last chapter, tried to imitate his father-in-law Theagenes, the tyrant of Megara, and seize power in Athens. The earliest records of this event vary in their details; Herodotus (5, 71) says that Cylon and his followers did not succeed in getting hold of the Acropolis, and that he paid for the attempt with his life. Thucydides gives a more detailed account (1, 126) according to which the conspirators did take the Acropolis, but did not hold it for long. 'Athenians from the country-side' hurried to the scene and although Cylon had military help from Megara, his position soon became untenable. He and his brother were said to have escaped, but his followers were surrounded. Some of them starved to death while those who sought sanctuary in the temple of the goddess Athena were mercilessly killed. The Athenian aristocrat Megacles, son of Alcmeon, was held responsible for this deed.

Cylon was a victor at the thirty-fifth Olympic Games (in 640 BC) and his attempt to become tyrant of Athens is said to have coincided with the Games, four years or more probably eight years later. It is obvious that the conspirators had no support among the people of Attica, but there seem to have been differences between the attitudes of various groups. Megacles was soon accused of having violated the right to sanctuary, and the Alcmeonids were more than once accused by their political opponents in later times, for the 'disgrace' of having killed the followers of Cylon. According to Herodotus the followers of Alcmeon broke the pledge given to the conspirators sheltering in the temple of Athena by 'the *prytans* of the *naucraries* who were administering Athens at that time.'

We learn from Aristotle's *Athenian Constitution* (8, 3) that each of the four phylae was split up into divisions of three *trittyes* ('thirds') and twelve naucraries, headed, according to him by the naucrari (*naukraroi*), who were in charge of the collection of taxes and the payment of expenses. The naucraries and naucrari (obviously identical with the prytans of the naucraries mentioned by Herodotus) are referred to in the laws drawn up by Solon. According to Julius Pollux (Polydeukes), the second century AD grammarian and orator, 'each naucrary sent two horsemen and one boat (Gr. *naus*), from which the name came.'

Some scholars have doubted whether the naucraries date from before the time of Solon. Herodotus' reference to the prytans of the naucraries has been used as an argument for bringing the date of Cylon's attempt to establish a tyranny — and therefore the reign of his father-in-law Theagenes in Megara — forward into the first half of the sixth century BC. This interpretation is quite out of keeping with the established chronology of Greek history in the seventh and sixth centuries BC, and has therefore not found acceptance. Equally unfounded were the attempts to derive the term 'naucrary' from other Greek words than *naus*, 'ship'. While it is true that in the seventh century Athens could not compete on the sea with the foremost colonizing city-states of Greece, ships are already found among the decorative motifs on Attic vessels of the Geometric style. At the end of the seventh century the Athenians were already able to win the battle for the island of Salamis, in which ships were essential. The existence of the naucraries thus corresponds to the stage of development of Athens at that time. They are also significant evidence that institutions based on the territorial principle with no bearing on clan relationships had already emerged within the tribal system.

Cylon's attempt to establish a tyranny, and the events which accompanied it, point to conflicts between different groups of eupatrids. The relatives of the followers of Cylon who had been killed demanded that the perpetrators of the crime, the followers of Megacles, should be punished, and tension grew in the state. It was in this situation that Dracon was charged with codification of customary law. We know little about the first of the Athenian lawmakers, but there can be no doubt as to his historical existence or the fact repeated by later historians, that Dracon completed the task entrusted to him during the thirty-ninth Olympiad, that is to say some time between 624 and 621 BC.

The fourth chapter of Aristotle's *Athenian Constitution* refers to constitutional measures which were attributed to Dracon, but the facts quoted there correspond not to conditions in archaic Greece, but to those known from classical times. Elsewhere in the same work (41, 2) Aristotle sums up the constitutional changes in the history of Athens from the earliest times up to the fourth century BC without mentioning Dracon's constitution. In his *Politics* he then explicitly says (2, 1274b 15) that Dracon 'gave laws to the constitution which was already in existence'. Although there are still attempts from time to time to prove that Dracon's constitution really existed, it is generally agreed that the account of this constitution dates only from the time of the Peloponnesian War. Analogous features with the constitution of 411 BC suggest that the conservatives who came to power at that time were trying to ensure prestige for the measures by which they wanted to curtail democracy in Athens.

It seems, then, that Dracon was the author of laws but not of the constitution. Classical writers stressed the severity of his laws, and a saying attributed to Demades, a fourth-century Athenian orator, is often quoted: that Dracon wrote his laws in blood, not ink. To this day harsh measures are called 'draconian'.

Dracon's laws dealt mainly with serious crimes; he made a distinction between murder and manslaughter. The latter was dealt with by the courts and the offender was protected from the vengeance of the dead man's relatives, but in cases of deliberate murder the right to avenge the victim was upheld. Certain other crimes, including theft and adultery, were also punished according to customary law. From the point of view of later practice, the punishment for these crimes (normally death) was very severe, but nevertheless Dracon's measures were important in that they codified legal practice.

Conflicts among the eupatrids were not the only sign of discord in Athens at this time. An even more serious problem was the growing tension between the aristocrats and the common people. At the very bottom of the scale were the bonded peasants, the hektemorioi, who were unable to meet their obligations to creditors especially after a bad harvest, and thus sank into slavery. The people of the cities were also discontented with existing conditions, and craftsmen and traders were no longer willing to tolerate the unlimited power assumed by the eupatrids. This was the situation at the beginning of the sixth century when Solon was appointed archon with the task of putting the state to rights.

Later tradition attributed legendary features to Solon, so that it is not easy to determine what he was really like and what he actually did. The most valuable source of information is his own writings, the surviving fragments of his poems and his laws. He came of an aristocratic family which claimed descent from the mythical King Codrus, the same family to which the later conservative statesman Critias belonged, one of the most powerful men in the government of the 'thirty tyrants' in Athens after the Peloponnesian War. On his mother's side the great Greek philosopher Plato also came of this family. Solon is said to have earned his popularity by persuading Megacles and his followers to appear before the judges and account for what they had done when suppressing Cylon and his fellow conspirators. Undoubtedly, however, Solon's active participation in the fighting over Salamis was a strong factor in his popularity.

Athens and Megara had long been in conflict over Salamis. In the early phase of the archaic period Megara had played a more important part in the Greek world than her northern neighbour, and been very active in colonizing both Sicily and the Black Sea straits. The Megarian fleet was anchored at Nisaea, and rounded the coast of Salamis on its way through the Saronic Gulf to the Aegean. It was of vital importance for Megara to control the island. The same could of course be said for Athens, for the southern coast of Attica lay in the immediate vicinity of Salamis, and the port of Phaleron and later Piraeus were built there. In the seventh century, though, the Athenians had no ports on the Saronic Gulf. Prasiae was on the little indented eastern coast of Attica, a long way from Athens. It was not surprising that as the production of olive oil and decorative pottery —the two principal articles of Athenian export—increased, it became more and more urgent to gain access to the Saronic Gulf.

The attempt by Cylon, son-in-law of Theagenes the tyrant of Megara, to seize power in Athens, seems to have been prompted by the Megarian need to maintain superiority in the area. When the rising was defeated the conflict between the two states intensified. According to a later tradition recorded by Plutarch in his *Life of Solon* (8), the Athenians were unsuccessful in their struggle against Megara and therefore passed a law instituting the death penalty for anyone

133

proposing that Salamis should be conquered. Solon is said to have pretended to be mad so as not to incur this penalty; he then wrote a poem of one hundred lines about Salamis and recited it before the people assembled in the Athenian Agora. He so roused their enthusiasm that they attacked the Megarians again, successfully this time, and gained Salamis.

The story of Solon's pretended madness seems to have derived from his own verses (fragment 23 in E. Diehl's edition) in which one of his political opponents called him mad for not seizing the chance to become tyrant of Athens. Some classical authors, including Herodotus (1, 59), attributed the Athenian victory over Megara to the tyrant Peisistratus. According to Plutarch (*Solon* 8) Peisistratus was one of those who was moved by Solon's verses to take part in the fighting for Salamis. It is not surprising that scholars differ in their accounts of the struggle between Megara and Athens, but Solon's active participation cannot be denied. Some lines of his elegy on Salamis have survived, including a passionate call to arms to win the island. It is of course likely that the Athenians' success was only temporary and that the struggle broke out again in the third quarter of the sixth century, under Peisistratus.

While Solon's part in the fighting for Salamis cannot be denied, it is doubtful whether he took part in the important campaign at the beginning of the sixth century, known as the First Sacred War. The people of Krisa, which lay on the road from the coast of Delphi, made use of their strategic position near the wealthy shrine to demand taxes from the pilgrims making for the famous temple of Apollo. Those city-states which belonged to the Pylian *amphictiony*, or league, came to the aid of the Delphic priests; the amphictiony was originally set up to protect the temple of Demeter at Anthele in the pass of Thermopylae. Some classical sources say that Solon took part in the First Sacred War against Krisa, while others (see Plutarch, *Solon* 11) maintain that the Athenians fighting alongside the other members of the amphictiony were led by Alcmeon, the son of Megacles, the man who had suppressed Cylon's rising.

It was not only on account of his military exploits over Salamis that

Solon was placed at the head of the state, but because he made a serious attempt to deal with the pressing internal problems of Athens. We can see this from some of the verse he wrote before he was made archon, and particularly from the elegiac poem 'Eunomia' (3; Diehl). Solon here criticizes those of his fellow-citizens who blindly pursue wealth and profit, as well as ambitious leaders of the people. He is grieved to see the poor sold into slavery abroad in such numbers, and fears that internal discord will ruin the state. In contrast to these conditions, which he calls 'lawlessness' (*dysnomia*) he gives the picture of a lawful order (*eunomia*) in which illegal actions are restrained and strife and discord resolved. Other lines written by Solon during this period are critical of miserliness and arrogance in the powerful, and call for decency and honourable behaviour.

Thus it was not by chance that Solon was called upon to deal with the crisis into which Athenian society had fallen. Most classical authors are agreed that he became archon in the third year of the forty-sixth Olympiad, that is 594/3 BC. We learn from Aristotle's *Athenian Constitution* (5,2) that in addition to holding the highest office in the state, Solon was made mediator (*diallaktes*) between the eupatrids and the people.

After taking office as archon, Solon declared all debts to be abolished, bought all Athenians out of slavery, and made it illegal for anyone to pledge his personal freedom to his creditors. The abolition of slavery for debt was of far-reaching importance for the economic development of Athens. No Athenian citizen could be sold into slavery because he could not meet his obligations, and even the poorest of them enjoyed the fundamental rights of citizenship. In one of his iambic poems (24; Diehl) Solon rightly considers this abolition of slavery for debt as one of his most significant actions.

It is not known how Solon carried out this plan in detail, how he found out where there were Athenians who had been sold into slavery abroad for their debts, or where he got the money with which to buy them back. Nor is it known how these people made a living when they returned to Attica, although it is very likely that they found employment in Athens, where the crafts were expanding rapidly.

We learn from this same poem that Solon got rid of the landmarks and thus freed the hektemorioi from their dependence on the rich landowners. In his *Athenian Constitution* (6, 1) Aristotle records that the abolition of debts and of slavery for debt was called *seisachtheia* ('shaking off the burden'). Later authors thought that Solon did not abolish all debts, but only lowered the rate of interest by means of changes in the system of weights and measures, and in the value of coinage. There was even an apocryphal anecdote according to which Solon and his friends managed to enrich themselves in the process, but such remarks were invented by later authors who saw seisachtheia with the eyes of their own time, and failed to understand its true significance.

At the turn of the seventh century BC the economy of Athens was still based on barter. Although the use of precious metals, especially silver, as a measure of value was already known, money was still in its infancy. In spite of some objections, the latest numismatic evidence leads us to conclude that the earliest Athenian coins date from as late as the second half of the sixth century. Solon could not therefore have had anything to do with changes in the Athenian coinage, as was commonly believed until quite recently. It is now being suggested that the classical tradition according to which Solon reorganized the system of weights and measures in Athens must also be regarded with scepticism.

Seisachtheia had a profound effect on the structure of Athenian society, making possible the evolution of a community of all the citizens of the state. This did not mean that all citizens enjoyed the same rights. Far from it; another significant measure taken by Solon was the constitutional division of all citizens into four categories according to the yield of their land. The lowest group were the *thetes* (landless labourers) including landless peasants and those whose annual harvest was not more than 200 medimni (units of 52 litres). The third group were the small farmers whose harvest exceeded 200 medimni; they were called *zeugitai*, presumably because they used yoke oxen to cultivate their land. The wealthier farmers whose harvest yielded from 300 to 500 medimni annually were called *hippeis* (horsemen). At the top of the scale were the wealthy citizens whose annual harvest was over 500 medimni and who were therefore called *pentakosiomedimnoi* (*pentakosioi* = 500). At least three of these names probably existed in Athens even before the time of Solon; the thetes are found in epic poetry. The term may have acquired greater significance at the period when a citizen army was formed in Athens, and the thetes served as light infantry, the zeugitai as hoplites, and the hippeis as cavalry.

The medimnus was the unit of loose weight, used primarily for grain. Liquids were measured in smaller units, the *metretai* being a vessel holding not quite 39 litres. Both Aristotle in the *Athenian Constitution* (7,4) and Plutarch in his *Life of Solon* (18) say, however, that the annual yield both in liquid and loose crops was calculated in medimni. The rights of the citizens of Athens were graduated according to which of the four classes they were placed in. The thetes were only allowed to sit in the assembly (*ekklesia*) and the courts of justice, while only members of the two highest groups could hold important posts. The treasurers and perhaps the archons as well were chosen from among the pentakosiomedimnoi. Thus the wealthiest citizens, the eupatrids, still remained the most powerful individuals in the state. Nevertheless Solon's constitution was of great importance; instead of high birth landed property was now the criterion.

Solon's timocratic constitution thus gave the basic political rights to all citizens alike, but entrusted the decisive influence in the state to the wealthy, to the great landowners. Solon himself in one of his poems (5, 1–6; Diehl) declared that his aim was to meet the wishes of the people without injuring the interests of those who hitherto held power in Athens.

Classical tradition also attributed to Solon the institution known as the 'council of 400', in which all four phylae were equally represented. We have no concrete information about how it worked, however. He left the council which traditionally met on the Areopagus, although under the new constitution it no longer consisted solely of aristocrats. What was the function of the council of 400? Some scholars believe that it was invented later, on analogy with the council of 500 established at the end of the sixth century by Cleisthenes, in which all the ten local phylae were equally represented. The question of this council of 400 is one of those still unanswered in the evolution of the Athenian state in the archaic period. Solon's constitution gave the people's assembly greater importance, and another significant institution, the *heliaia* ('jury'), was closely linked with it.

The laws of Solon were inscribed on rotating wooden slabs (*axones*) and their authority persisted into the classical age. Many writers quote and refer to individual laws and other measures taken by Solon, and Athenian tradition often attributes to Solon laws which were decidedly of later date. Critical analysis of the material, however, allows us to form a reliable picture of the character and content of Solon's legal measures. As we have already seen, Solon took over Dracon's ruling concerning murder and manslaughter, but some traces of the right to carry on a blood-feud also persisted. Solon instituted less drastic penalties than Dracon for offences against private property. Details of the laws dealing with various moral offences have come down to us, as well as satisfaction for defamation. Questions of family and inheritance including adoption played a large part in Solon's code. He also instituted measures aimed at reducing extravagance, laid down detailed regulations for land tenure and for the mutual relationship between neighbours. The law by which every Athenian could demand satisfaction for wrongs inflicted by a fellow-citizen shows the growing significance of civil rights. Evidence given by witnesses was of great importance during the hearing of a case. Besides offences against individuals, measures were taken against those who threatened the stability of the state, especially conspiracy to set up a tyranny. Of particular interest is the law concerning the granting of civil rights to foreigners who had settled in Athens, which explicitly refers to craftsmen who had immigrated there. Both the seisachtheia and the constitution were duly codified.

The measures taken by Solon were an important factor in the evolution of the Athenian city-state, and had far-reaching consequences for Athenian society. His measures were accepted by the Athenians, who gave their solemn pledge that they would abide by them. Not that they were all content; in his verse Solon defends himself and argues against some of his critics. He repeatedly claims to have tried to satisfy the demands of the people without damaging the interests of the aristocrats.

Soon after his term of office ended, Solon went abroad, and the discontent which had been coming to the surface during his rule broke out into open conflict. According to Aristotle (*Athenian Constitution* 13, 1-2) these disagreements were the reason why it was twice impossible to elect an archon at all. Then Damasias became archon, and refused to relinquish his post for two years and two months, until violence was used to remove him from power. Finally the difficulty was overcome by the decision to elect 'ten archons, five chosen from the eupatrids, three from the *agroikoi* and two from the *demiourgoi*, and these archons then governed for the year after Damasias'. According to the chronology given by Aristotle, this happened in 580/79 BC. This compromise suggests that there was tension between the different social groups.

In addition to the conflicts which arose from social differences, Athens seems to have suffered again from hostility between rival groups of eupatrids. Classical writers speak of three groups (*staseis*, 'parties') struggling to hold power in the city state; these were the inhabitants of the plain of Attica (*pedion*), who were called *pediakoi* or *pedieis*, the people of the coastal region (*paralia*) called *paralioi* or *paraloi*, and the people of the mountains, known as *diakrioi* or *hyperakrioi*. Earlier scholars identified the pediakoi with eupatrid landowners, the paralioi with the peasants or more often with the merchants and craftsmen, and the diakrioi with shepherds and landless peasants. There were even suggestions that the diakrioi were miners working in the Attic silver mines at Laurium. This interpretation is based on the division of the populace adopted by Aristotle in keeping with his idea of three types of government: oligarchy, (moderate) constitutional government (*politeia*) and democracy.

Research has since shown that the decisive men in each of the groups struggling to gain power were the eupatrids who wielded influence in the different parts of Attica. I do not think the conflicts can be reduced simply to hostility between different eupatrid clans. Herodotus records (1, 59) that when the pediakoi and paralioi were engaged in a struggle for power, Peisistratus wanted to become a tyrant and set up a stasis drawn from the hyperakrioi. He seems to have found his support among the discontented elements in Athens, perhaps the landless. As we know from Solon's verses, it was between the people and the eupatrids that feelings ran high. The information at our disposal is not sufficient to form a clear idea of the nature of the conflict as a whole, but it seems to have compounded both the struggle for power between different groups of eupatrids and the social antagonisms between different strata of Athenian citizens.

According to Herodotus the pediakoi were led by Lycurgus, son of Aristolaidas, while Megacles, the son of Alcmeon, led the paralioi. It is not impossible that the old hostility between the two, dating from the time when the Alcmeonids crushed the conspiracy of Cylon, was behind the conflict; the family, one of the most important among the aristocracy, still nourished political ambitions. Alcmeon led the Athenian contingent in the Sacred War against Krisa. Megacles, the leader of the paralioi, married to Agariste, daughter of Cleisthenes, tyrant of Sicyon, was one of the most powerful men in Athens. Peisistratus, whose family claimed descent from the mythical ruler of Pylos, Nestor, was very popular; he seems to have profited from his success in the new outbreak of fighting between Athens and Megara, when he not only renewed Athenian control of the island of Salamis, but gained the port of Nisaea as well. On the grounds that he had been attacked and knocked down by political opponents he was allowed a bodyguard, and with their help he seized the Acropolis and became tyrant, probably in 561/60 BC. His rule did not last long, however, the pediakoi and the paralioi joining forces to get rid of him.

Peisistratus did not give up, however. He made an alliance with Megacles and married the latter's daughter, and with the help of the paralioi he again became tyrant of Athens. According to Herodotus (1, 60) he came to power without using force this time; disguising a tall and beautiful young woman as the goddess Athena, he placed her on a chariot in full armour. 'Then they drove into the city, sending messengers before them to spread what they were told to say: "People of Athens, rejoice and welcome Peisistratus," they cried, "whom Athena herself has honoured above all men, bringing him back to her Acropolis". They went about the city saying this, and the rumour spread throughout the city that Athena herself was bringing Peisistratus back. The people of the town believed that the young woman was the goddess herself, and prayed to her and welcomed Peisistratus.'

Even after this manoeuvre Peisistratus did not manage to hold on to power for long. He quarrelled with Megacles, according to the version given by both Herodotus and Aristotle, because he did not wish to have children by his new wife, which Megacles took as a personal affront. Peisistratus could not stay in power without the support of the paralioi, and this time he was forced to leave not only Athens but Attica altogether. He settled first in Macedonia and then in south-west Thrace, where he worked silver mines on Mount Pangaeum in order to finance another attempt to seize power in Athens. This time he secured military support from some of the Greek city-states, particularly Euboean Eretria and Boeotian Thebes. Lygdamis of the island of Naxos was also on his side; he himself would have liked to institute a tyranny, and therefore saw in Peisistratus a welcome ally.

Peisistratus took great pains to prepare his third attempt to seize power; first he moved his army from Eretria into Attica and seized Marathon, and from there moved against Athens. He defeated the Athenian army in a decisive battle, and could at last take his place as a tyrant. It is difficult to determine the separate phases of the campaign, but it is most probable that the decisive battle, which ensured his success, occurred in 546/5 BC.

141

Classical tradition describes the reign of Peisistratus, like that of other tyrants in the archaic period, in fairly favourable terms. Herodotus commented (1, 59) that Peisistratus 'did not abolish offices or abrogate laws, but ruled in accordance with the existing laws, and administered the polis fairly and well'. The description in Aristotle's *Athenian Constitution* — in two places in fact (14,3 and 16,2) — agrees with this attitude, commenting that Peisistratus governed in a 'civil way (*politikōs*) rather than as a tyrant'. In his *Life of Solon* (30) Plutarch praised Peisistratus for having 'maintained many of the laws of Solon'.

The tyrant of Athens took good care to protect himself against possible rebels. According to Herodotus (1, 64) 'he took as hostages the sons of those citizens of Athens who did not flee at once but stayed in the country; he sent them to Naxos, having conquered the island by war and entrusted it to Lygdamis'. Some of the opponents of Peisistratus fell in the fighting and others, headed by Megacles, left Athens in time and sought refuge in other Greek states. It is often suggested that Peisistratus confiscated the lands of these emigrants and distributed it among the landless peasants of his following, but there is no evidence for this in the sources. All that Aristotle says (*Athenian Constitution* 16, 3–5) is that Peisistratus encouraged agriculture in Attica, appointing district judges and often coming in person to settle difficult cases. This was apparently in order to prevent the peasants from coming into Athens; he tried to keep them 'scattered through the countryside, to give them a decent living, so that they would keep their minds on their own affairs and have neither the time nor the desire to meddle in public affairs'.

Agriculture was a source of considerable income for Peisistratus, who received tithes from the harvest. Under the tyranny the crafts and trade also flourished, however, and study of Attic black figure vases has shown that most finds of this excellent pottery from the workshops of Athens date from the period 560–520 BC, that is largely from the reign of Peisistratus. This evidence of the material culture of the time also testifies to lively contacts between Athens and Asia Minor, Cyprus, the Black Sea region and especially Etruria.

142

There were well-known craftsmen working in the Athenian potteries, like the potter Ergotimos and the painter Kleitias, the creators of the famous François Vase (c.570); the painter Lydos and the potter and painter Exekias, who was one of the great masters of black figure pottery; and many more whose names still live on the pottery that came from their hands.

At the beginning of the second half of the sixth century BC a new style began to emerge in Athens. Instead of black figures on the natural (pale) clay surface, a new technique, using the light red colour of the clay for the figures against the black painted background, gave greater opportunity to the artist to endow his figures with expression. By the end of the sixth century red figure pottery predominated in Athens, and persisted long into the classical period. Under Peisistratus and later under the tyranny of his sons there were great masters making vases in this style, like the potter Andokides and the unknown painter who worked with him (known as Andokides' painter), the elder Epictetos, and many others.

In the second half of the sixth century the centre of the Athenian pottery workshops, Kerameikos, grew into a large urban quarter. Dedicatory inscriptions set up on the Acropolis by potters particularly in the last third of the century also testify to the increasing importance of the craft in Athens at this time. The potteries did not only produce the magnificent vases, beautifully decorated and of various shapes, which served mainly ornamental purposes; they also made vessels for everyday use, including the large amphorae and barrels in which agricultural produce was transported, especially the wine and olive oil for which Attica was already famous.

Under Peisistratus, or rather under his sons, important building went on in Athens. The large water reservoir known as Enneakrounos ('of nine springs') was constructed then, and the pipes, which carried water to Kerameikos and still provided some of the Athens water supply in modern times, also date from the second half of the sixth century BC. A temple to the goddess Athena was built on the Acropolis, known as the Hecatompedon because of its length ('a hundred feet').

Money to finance these expensive investments came not only from land taxes, but from the silver mines in Laurium. Archaeological research has proved that mining began earlier, but reached considerable proportions in the second half of the sixth century. Besides landless free men there were slaves working in the mines, brought to Athens mainly from the eastern regions. Slaves from Asia Minor, and especially from the northern shores of the Black Sea, were also put to work digging potters' clay, and probably in the potteries as well.

When the Athenians gained control of the port of Nisaea, they brought to a successful conclusion a struggle of many years' standing to wrest the island of Salamis from Megara and thus to gain access to the Saronic Gulf and the Aegean. Peisistratus was not content to control Naxos; in his account of how the tyrant of Athens put Lygdamis to rule over Naxos, Herodotus added (1, 64) that he 'cleared the island of Delos, too, in accordance with the oracles'. Thucydides (1, 104, 1−2) records the same fact. Peisistratus was also concerned to strengthen the position of the Athenians in the Hellespont, where they had been fighting Mytilene over Sigeum as early as the end of the seventh century. Success here seems to have led to Athenian expansion in Thracian Chersonese. We learn from Herodotus (6, 34−8) that it was Miltiades of the aristocratic Philaid family, uncle of the later Marathon victor of the same name, who seized Chersonese. Thus Peisistratus got rid of a dangerous rival at home and Athens gained control over the Hellespont. Finds of Attic black figure and red figure pottery in the Black Sea colonies testify to the growing influence of Athens in the region.

In addition to furthering the economic prosperity and political power of Athens, Peisistratus did much to strengthen the internal stability of the state. As under Solon, the cult of the goddess Athena was again in the forefront, symbolizing the unanimity of the citizen body. The quadrennial Great Panathenaea took place in honour of the goddess, competing with the festivities in honour of Zeus at Olympia in Elis and those in honour of Apollo at Delphi. The Homeric epics were recited at the Panathenaea, and it seems to have been at this time that passages celebrating the ancient history of the city were interpolated. The cult of Athena also found expression in the type of coins minted either under Peisistratus or, more probably, under his sons; the head of the goddess on the obverse, and her attributes — the owl and the olive sprig — on the reverse, marked the Athenian silver *tetradrachm* which soon earned a good reputation in the Greek world. Besides Athena, Dionysus was worshipped, particularly by the common people. Tragic choruses were performed at the City Dionysia, at the beginning of every spring, and from this Attic drama evolved, one of the greatest expressions of Greek culture. A later tradition has it that Thespis was the creator of the tragic choruses, at the time of the sixty-first Olympiad (536–533 BC), i.e. during the tyranny of Peisistratus.

According to Aristotle (*Athenian Constitution* 16,7), Athenian tradition compared the tyranny of Peisistratus to the golden age of Kronos, but his sons ruled much more harshly. At first, however, Hippias and Hipparchus seem to have carried on their father's policy when they assumed the tyranny on his death in 528/7 BC. They even seem to have been reconciled with some of their political opponents, judging from a late fifth-century inscription found in the Agora of Athens and published in 1939. The fragment gives part of a list of archons, in which three successive names can be deciphered: Hippias, Cleisthenes and Miltiades. Since it was already known that Miltiades — the Marathon victor rather than his uncle of the same name — was archon in 524/3, it is clear that Hippias, the eldest son of Peisistratus, held the office in 526/5, shortly after becoming the tyrant of Athens, and that for 525/4 the archon was Cleisthenes of the Alcmeonids, the son of Megacles and Agariste, called after his grandfather the famous tyrant of Sicyon.

The sons of Peisistratus invited well-known Greek poets to Athens. According to Aristotle (18, 1) Hippias dealt with the business of government while Hipparchus preferred the pleasanter things of life; he it was who 'invited Anacreon, Simonides and the other poets to Athens'. Their extravagant and pleasure-loving life landed the sons of Peisistratus in financial difficulties, and led them to take unpopular measures which heightened the discontent of the citizens of Athens, directing it against the tyranny. We know from the history of other Greek states that this form of government, aimed at increasing the stability of the city-state (polis) and weakening the power of the aristocratic families, rarely lasted long. The emergent social forces soon began to feel that the tyranny was standing in the way of further economic and political progress, and to try to remove it. In Athens the opposition took the form of assassination, and the victim was Hipparchus.

The date was 514 BC, during the Great Panathenaea, and in later Athenian tradition Harmodius and Aristogeiton, who organized the plot, were celebrated as liberators. Statues of the 'tyrannicides' were set up in the Athenian agora, and verses in their honour were recited at banquets. Yet Herodotus was already commenting, in two passages (5, 55; 6, 123), that the assassination of Hipparchus did not abolish tyranny in Athens; on the contrary, the regime became even more oppressive. Thucydides in two separate places (1, 20; 6, 54) reproached the Athenians for mistakenly honouring Harmodius and Aristogeiton as their liberators, when they were in fact only acting out of personal enmity towards Hipparchus. Aristotle (*Athenian Constitution* 18, 2–5) gives a similar picture of the background to the assassination but adds that besides the hostility aroused by Hipparchus, his younger brother Thessalus was the cause of much animosity. It was said that many Athenians were involved in the plot, and that it was aimed primarily at Hippias.

Whatever the sequence of events surrounding the assassination, it is probable that besides personal motives the growing opposition to the tyranny played an important role. The murder of Hipparchus did not profit the conspirators much; on the contrary, Hippias took strong measures against his real and supposed enemies. It was now the turn of emigrants to take the initiative against tyranny in Athens. Cleisthenes was foremost among them, apparently having left Athens soon after his reconciliation with Peisistratus. Changes in the region of the Aegean had weakened the position of Hippias; the Persians were not content just to control the Greek cities in Asia Minor, but were trying to overrun other parts of the Greek world.

The first to fall was Samos, which had been one of the most powerful Greek states under Polycrates; then came Naxos, and with the fall of the tyrant Lygdamis Hippias lost one of his most devoted allies. The Athenian aristocrats who had long before been sent to Naxos as hostages by Peisistratus were now at liberty and joined forces with the enemies of the Athenian tyrant. His position grew even weaker when the Persians penetrated the Hellespont and took Sigeum and occupied the Thracian Chersonese.

The first attempt to overthrow the tyranny of the sons of Peisistratus by force was unsuccessful. The exiled aristocrats moved into Attica from Boeotia and encamped not far from the border, at Leipsydrion, where they were joined by a number of Athenians from the city. Hippias surrounded Leipsydrion with his army and forced them to retreat. It was clear that they would need a strong ally if they were to succeed. The Alcmeonids got the Delphic Pythia (oracle giver) on their side, who is said to have constantly urged the Spartans to overthrow the tyrant of Athens. Hippias was not idle, however, and provided himself with armed reinforcements from Thessaly.

The Spartans do not seem to have needed much persuading to attack Hippias. As is well known, it was Spartan policy to support conservative regimes and therefore to oppose tyranny. As the hegemony of the Peloponnesian League was in the hands of Sparta, she controlled most of southern Greece, and was anxious to extend her power. The attack on Hippias turned out to be unexpectedly difficult, however, and the Spartan contingent that landed at Phaleron was defeated. A stronger force sent overland under King Cleomenes I succeeded in scattering the Thessalian cavalry and penetrated into Attica, to lay siege to Hippias on the Acropolis. When the children of the Peisistratid family were captured as they tried to escape secretly from Athens, the tyrant capitulated; in 511/10 BC he retired to Sigeum, then under Persian control.

Once their common enemy was defeated, the two opposing groups in Athens began a furious struggle. The one led by Isagoras was supported by conservative eupatrid circles and could rely on Spartan aid, while the second was led by the Alcmeonids, with

Cleisthenes at their head. This experienced statesman knew that his only chance of weakening his opponents was to gain the support of the majority of the Athenians. According to Herodotus (5, 66) when Cleisthenes felt he was losing he 'gained the favour of the people', and we find a similar report in Aristotle's *Athenian Constitution* (20, 1). Isagoras did not give up, however, and called on the Spartan King Cleomenes I for help. With the Spartans behind him he was able to have the Alcmeonids again declared 'unclean' because of the killing of the followers of Cylon. Cleisthenes secretly fled from Athens and Cleomenes started to send his followers into exile. Athens was to be governed by 300 Athenian aristocrats headed by Isagoras, and thus to come under Spartan influence. The Athenian council (presumably the Areopagus) objected to this proposal, and the people of Athens surrounded Cleomenes and Isagoras on the Acropolis. They were forced to capitulate and to leave the country, whereupon Cleisthenes and his followers were brought back.

The people of Athens had finally decided for themselves the way their state was to follow, and Cleisthenes seized the opportunity to institute far-reaching administrative reforms. The basis was the formation of ten local phylae, which meant that the previous division into four Ionian phylae and the phratries lost its political significance. The new local divisions were not laid down mechanically, however; Attica was divided into three regions, the coastal region, the inland, and the urban (embracing the town and its immediate vicinity). Each of the ten new phylae consisted of one third (*trittys*) coastal elements, one third from the inland, and one third from the town. This completely broke up the old relationships, which had made it easy for the aristocrats to maintain their privileged position in the city-state. The new arrangement, destroying the influence of the old tribal divisions, made it possible for all citizens to be equal before the law (*isonomia*), the principle from which Athenian democracy evolved in the classical period.

The local phylae were divided into *demoi*, usually corresponding each to one Attic village, or several small neighbouring ones; in Athens the demoi corresponded to the quarters of the city. The demoi were made up of individuals, however, and were not a unit of territorial administration. Lists of citizens were drawn up according to the demoi, and in the process — as under Solon — citizenship was also granted to some foreigners. The naucraries, which were the first form of local organization, lost their significance. The fact that a man's antecedents were usually given according to which deme he belonged to, and not which family, also contributed to make all men equal before the law.

A new council (*boule*) of 500 was also established, based on the local phylae, which were equally represented. Every year the citizens of each deme elected their representatives to the council, by drawing lots. The members of the council of each phyle, known as the prytans, took turns in administering the current affairs of the city, in such a way that each phyle was 'in office' for one tenth of the year, while the chairman of the officiating prytans (*epistates*) sat only for one day. No citizen could become a member of the council of 500 more than twice in his lifetime. This was meant to ensure the broadest possible participation of all citizens in the administration of the state. Although our information about the work of the council of 500 refers to a later time, and although the Areopagus and the archons enjoyed great authority in Athens during the early phase of the classical period, the principal features of the election system and the function of the council date from Cleisthenes. Even the archons were appointed according to the local phylae, and a tenth member was added, the scribe of the *thesmothetai*. Ten military commanders were elected each year, the *strategoi*, and later became more important than the archons. The council of 500 studied in advance the proposals which were then put before the assembly (*ekklesia*), and it had the right to advise officials.

Classical tradition also links the introduction of ostracism with the name of Cleisthenes. The earliest instance dates from the eighties of the fifth century, but it is very likely that the custom was indeed instituted by Cleisthenes. Every year the citizens of Athens had the right to inscribe on a clay shard (*ostrakon*) the name of the man they thought a threat to the security of the community, and who ought therefore to be sent into exile for ten years. The sentence was only carried out if at least 6,000 citizens agreed on the same name. Ostracism was intended as a protection against the recurrence of tyranny.

All these reforms, and particularly the establishment of the complicated regional organizational measures, must have taken a considerable time, and they were not accomplished without trouble. The situation became more difficult in Athens when King Cleomenes I, urged by Isagoras, again attempted military intervention in 506 BC. He was met by opposition from his Corinthian allies, according to Herodotus (5, 75), as well as from the other Spartan king, Demaratus. The Athenians were well able to deal with the Boeotians and the Chalcidians who attacked Attica from the north. After this victory Cleisthenes completed his programme of reforms. Scholars have tried to determine the chronological sequence of his reforms, but all that can be stated with certainty is that they lasted several years and were not completed until right at the end of the sixth century.

In spite of all the changes and reversals in the course of the archaic period, Athenian society moved gradually away from a tribal organization controlled by the eupatrids to a highly developed city-state based on a firm constitution and administered according to agreed principles. Although individuals of high birth continued to play an important part in city affairs, it was no longer as the representatives of the aristocratic clans, but of the community as a whole. Naturally social differences between the citizens persisted, but all Athenian citizens were subject to the same laws and took part in the administration of their state. The constitution of Cleisthenes opened the way to the democratic regime in the Athens of Pericles' day.

CHAPTER VI

Art, Literature and Thought in Archaic Greece

While the Greek economy developed by leaps and bounds during the archaic period, accompanied by revolutionary social and political change, Greek culture was maturing. There is a wealth of material evidence, as well as literary remains.

As a rule the finest works of art are closely bound up with religion. In many respects the Greeks of the archaic period continued the religious traditions of the Mycenaean Achaeans. Unlike them however, they did not make their worship of the gods subordinate to the social structure of palace rule and the authority of the king, but created new forms of ritual. Local tribal groups in the course of an involved historical development began to form a citizen body grouped into a polis and to set up temples dedicated to the deities on whom they relied for protection. Great temples were also built on the site of traditional religious ceremony, around which more than one city would be grouped (amphictyonies).

A Greek temple was not the place where believers gathered to worship, but the 'home' of the god, in which his statue was placed along with the treasures offered him. Sacrifice was made on an altar placed in front of the temple building. The architecture of the temple grew out of the typical Greek house, the *megaron*, and in the earliest times timber was the material used. Later, when stone was used, a number of features still recalled the original material; besides the columns, which had originally been hewn tree trunks, the treatment of the beams and the roof showed the clearest traces of this. These elements were particularly marked in the style which is known as the Doric order, where the characteristic feature is a frieze arranged in *triglyphs*, which evolved from the jutting ends of three roof beams, and *metopes*, which were originally formed by terracotta revetment covering the space between the timbers. The metopes and the triangular pediment (the *tympanon*) formed the ground for sculptural ornament. In the architecture of the Ionic order, which evolved in the islands of the Aegean and on the west coast of Asia Minor, the heritage of Cretan civilization was more evident, as well as the influence of the cultures of the Near East. The Ionic order was lighter, with slender pillars and more colourful ornament particularly in the continuous bands of the frieze. In the first half of the sixth century BC the Aeolic order developed, as a variant of the Ionic, characterized particularly by more articulated capitals. Corinthian capitals, the main feature of a style developed during the classical period, were elaborate and flower-shaped.

One of the earliest temples, with the typical colonnade, was that dedicated to Hera on the island of Samos. A timber-built temple was erected here as early as the beginning of the eighth century BC, on the site of an ancient shrine. The Heraion on Samos was rebuilt several times in the archaic period, and from the middle of the seventh century stone gradually took the place of timber and terracotta. The temple which was erected during the tyranny of Polycrates was remarkably majestic in proportions, with large numbers of columns. The temple of Hera on the island of Delos was built around the year 630 BC and in the sanctuary of Apollo on Delos temples were set up during the sixth century by the citizens of Naxos and later those of other Aegean islands. The temple of Artemis in Ephesus could compare with, or even perhaps surpassed, the Heraion on Samos; here the Ionic order reached its supreme expression and displayed the most magnificent ornamentation. The archaic temple in Didyma near Miletus was destroyed by the Persians in 494 BC when they crushed the revolt of the Greeks in Asia Minor.

On the Greek mainland the evolution of temple buildings from the eighth to the seventh century can be traced in Aetolian Thermon, and the temple of Hera not far from Argos also had an ancient tradition; here timber was replaced by stone towards the end of the seventh century. It was at this time that the greatest temple on the Isthmus of Corinth was built; the temple of Apollo in Corinth dates from the second half of the sixth century, but a temple of Artemis with a richly ornamented pediment was erected on the island of Corcyra as early as under the tyranny of Periander (end of the seventh century). The Corinthians built their treasury at Delphi during this period, too. The temple of Athene at Delphi dates from the turn of the seventh century, while during the sixth century the number of religious edifices erected in the sanctuary of Apollo at Delphi by the different cities (Sicyon, Cnidus, Siphnos, Massalia) increased considerably. About the year 520 BC the Alcmeonids of Athens built a temple at Delphi, when they were preparing their revolt against the tyranny of Hippias.

The temple of Athena on the Acropolis of Athens was built in the first half of the sixth century. We have already referred to the building projects of the tyrants of Athens, in the chapter on the history of the city. In addition to the Hecatompedon, the sons of Peisistratus started the construction of the temple of Olympian Zeus, east of the Acropolis, but it was not finished until the reign of the emperor Hadrian. Other important buildings were erected in Attica in the archaic period, like the famous shrine at Eleusis (the *telesterion*) where the mysteries were held, and at the turn of the sixth century the earlier temple of Poseidon on Cape Sunium was built.

In Laconia the Spartan temple dedicated to Artemis Orthia had a very old tradition, going right back to the ninth century. The remains of a sixth century building have been found there. The foundations of the temple of Apollo not far away, at Amyclae, are also of the sixth century. The most important religious centre in the Peloponnese was of course Olympia, where the temple of Hera was soon the dominating feature; elements of the tradition of timber architectonics persisted here for a long time, in the form of oak columns. Already in archaic times the all-Greek character of the Olympian sanctuary of Zeus was seen in the treasuries built there by citizens from Greek colonies in the west (Gela, Metapontum) and in the east (Byzantium).

The temples of Apollo in North African Cyrene and in Egyptian Naucratis date from the first half of the sixth century, and the rapidly prospering colonies on Sicily and in southern Italy built temples which are still counted among the finest Greek architectural achievements of the archaic period. One of the finest sites is that of Selinus, where the earliest temple came into existence before the middle of the sixth century. In Syracuse the temple of Zeus also dates from this time, although the temple of Apollo is even earlier. In the course of the sixth century more temples were built in Selinus, and some very fine metopes with relief carvings of high quality have survived. At the turn of the sixth century work was begun on the temple of Olympian Zeus at Acragas. Among the finest monuments of archaic architecture in southern Italy are the temples at Poseidonia (Paestum), in particular the earlier temple of Hera known as the 'Basilica'. It was built about 530 BC, at the same time as the construction of the temple of Apollo in Metapontum and the temple of Artemis in Massalia.

Buildings dating from the first quarter of the fifth century are still archaic in style, as are the sculptures and paintings of that period. The temple of the goddess Aphaea on the island of Aegina and the treasury erected in Delphi by the Athenians after the Battle of Marathon are among the greatest achievements of archaic Doric order, but they no longer fit into the chronology of the early phase of Greek history, which is usually said to have ended at the turn of the sixth century. The Persian wars are already on the threshold of the classical period.

Sculpture, like architecture, was closely bound up with religious ideas. Small figurines of terracotta, and in rare cases of ivory, continue the Cretan-Mycenaean tradition; they represent goddesses and served as simple votive gifts. Clay figurines were made by potters in imitation of the metal statues.

Metal statues of warriors, usually in bronze, began to appear early in the archaic period, made by smiths and smelters. Small votive figurines of lead were also popular, as attested by archaeological excavation of the Spartan temple of Artemis Orthia. They date from the late seventh and early sixth centuries, and represent goddesses, warriors, flute-players and lyre-players, and various animals.

From the end of the seventh century, besides normal casting, a more economical process was used for the bronze figurines, in which the trunk, in particular, was formed by beating thin leaf metal on a wooden core. By the second half of the sixth century the *cire-perdue* technique had been mastered, which was much more sophisticated. The core was plastered with a thin layer of wax under the fire-resistant mould, which was fired normally, so that the wax melted and trickled out through a hole in the mould, the intervening space being then filled with melted bronze. After cooling the clay mould was removed.

Besides the small figurines of clay and metal, the seventh century saw the first larger sculptures in stone, at first on Crete, where tradition linked them with the name of the mythical architect of the palace of Knossos, Daedalus. These Daedalic statues are for the most part female portraits, the figures of goddesses and priestesses retaining the character of the block of stone from which they have been chiselled, while at the same time the wooden ritual statues, known only from later literary sources, have also left their mark.

Temple architecture provided archaic sculptors with a significant stimulus; pediments and friezes (or metopes) on the temples were inspired by mythical subjects. The pediment over the temple of Artemis on Corcyra, dating from the sixth century, represents Perseus fighting the Gorgon. A very popular theme was that of the Greek hero conquering a barbarian monster, as we can see on the metope of one of the temples of Selinus dating from the second half of the sixth century. Before the middle of the sixth century the relief carving on the pediment of the temple of Athena on the Athenian

Acropolis was executed, presenting scenes from the Heracles myth, in one of which the three-bodied snake-tailed monster is depicted. The metopes of the treasury of Sicyon at Delphi reveal the anti-Dorian tendencies which persisted in this city even after the fall of Cleisthenes' tyranny. A frequent motif which symbolized the struggle of the Greeks against the barbarians was seen in *Gigantomachy*, the representation of the victorious struggle of the Olympian gods against the previous generation of gods, the Giants. An archaic example of the theme can be seen on the frieze decorating the treasury erected by the citizens of the island of Siphnos at Delphi in 525 BC. Other mythical themes were also used here, particularly Trojan themes, while the pediment illustrates Heracles and Apollo fighting over the Delphic tripod. The magnificent work of these artists reflects not only Ionian traditions, but those of the mature art of the sculptors of Athens at that time.

Polychrome was a characteristic feature of relief carvings, which were coloured after completion. This technique was also used on free-standing statues of marble or limestone, and red was the predominant colour.

Towards the end of the seventh century human figures began to appear in sculpture, especially the figure of a naked youth (*kouros*, 'young man'), which was the expression of the ideal anthropomorphic god (Apollo) or man (the aristocrat). It represents a combination of the worship of the Olympian gods in human form which was so typical of Greek religious thought, with the cult of the dead and with the idealization of the 'beautiful and good' hero (*kalos kai agathos*). The fixed stance of the kouros with one foot thrust forward derives from the Geometric figurines of warriors, and the further development of the type can be seen in the classical figures of athletes. Unlike the statues of classical times, which are known chiefly from Roman copies, archaic kouroi have been found in their original strata during excavations, and are therefore original figures. Another common type of statue in archaic times was the figure of a girl (*kore*) in a pleated robe, a combination of the ideal of the goddess and her maidens — the priestesses.

Different tendencies can be traced in the portrait statuary of archaic Greece, and 'schools' relating to the different cities can be defined. Portrayal of the kouroi differs, for example, in that the Dorian type prefers muscular athletic proportions while the Ionian type presents more slender bodies with more rounded and delicate contours.

Typical of the Dorian type are the statues of the twins Cleobis and Biton dedicated to the Delphi sanctuary by the citizens of Argos at the beginning of the sixth century. They were carved in local limestone by the sculptor Polymedes. According to the legend the brothers harnessed themselves to their mother's chariot when she had no draught animals and, as a priestess of Hera, needed to travel to the famous temple of the goddess, about 8 kilometres (5 miles) from Argos. When Cydippe asked Hera to reward her sons for their devotion, the goddess sent death to them in their sleep. Cleobis and Biton, who thus perished at the summit of fame, were a model of youthful strength, unselfishness and piety. In the famous fictitious meeting between Solon and Croesus, first noted by Herodotus (1, 31), the Athenian law-giver quoted the two youths as a model of the happy life, to be imitated. The two statues testify to the links between the Daedalic statuary and the figures of kouroi.

A typical example of Ionian statuary is the kouros from Melos, dating from the middle of the sixth century. A somewhat older Ionian statue is the rounded figure of Hera with rich drapery, from Samos. Figures of goddesses and rulers, seated, the contours of the human form merging with the drapery, were very popular. Seventy sixth-century statues were found along the sacred path to the temple of Apollo in Didyma near Miletus; they portray aristocrats of the clan of the Branchidae, who traditionally occupied the highest priestly offices in the temple.

There were archaic 'schools' of sculpture on Naxos, in Sparta, in Corinth and in other cities, and Corinthian influence can be traced in the statuary from Greek colonies in Sicily and southern Italy. Here, too, Ionian features are evident, but the strongest influence is that of local traditions, which give a specific character to the work that was produced here.

Gradually Athens began to lead the way in sculpture. The statue of the Calf-Bearer, found on the Acropolis in 1864, dates from after 570 BC. The figure of the so-called Rampin Horseman, which like the preceding statue was carved in honour of the goddess Athena, is about ten years later. Both figures were undoubtedly donated by wealthy Athenian citizens, probably aristocrats. In style the figure of the Horseman is very close to that of a young woman in another statue, usually called the Peplos Kore and probably dating from after 540 BC. In contrast to the richly draped figures in the Ionian tradition, the young girl is clad in the simple Dorian *peplos*, which displays the contours of the body to better advantage.

Figures of girls (korai) were very popular in Athens in the late sixth and early fifth centuries; several dozen have been preserved, many still bearing traces of polychrome. They were most probably votive gifts presented to Athena by maidens of the foremost Athenian families, who had the honour of weaving the robes for the statue of the goddess. The group of figures depicting Athena attacking a Giant, from the east pediment of the Hecatompedon, is an important example of the art of portraiture in archaic Athens; it dates from about 520 BC.

The skill of the Athenian sculptors also found expression on funeral steles, of which Aristion's, dating from the end of the sixth century, is the finest example. The technical mastery shown in the surviving statuary, and the realistic portrayal of the human body, testify to the place of Athens in the arts, besides her position in the forefront of social and political evolution in archaic Greece. The art of vase painting, too, confirms this predominance.

Like architecture and sculpture, painting also advanced during the archaic period. We have already seen how Greek artists used a great deal of colour when putting the finishing touches to their statues. In earlier times the space between the triglyphs on the friezes of Doric temples was filled with terracotta slabs on which mythical scenes were painted; flat metopes of this kind have survived in the temple of Apollo at Thermon in Aetolia. There were paintings on terracotta ornamenting the walls of buildings, but we only know these from

158

Etruscan finds, where the Greek influence is apparent. The evolution
of Greek painting can be followed in the development of painted
vases.

Vase painting, of course, was closely bound up with the art of the
potter. The Greeks used the word *techne* ('art', 'skill') to describe the
work of both painter and potter, respecting the potter's above the
painter's art. This may have been due to the complicated processes
involved particularly in the firing of clay vessels, where the skill and
craftsmanship of the potters came into their own. Pottery was a
common product in Greece, used for many purposes, from the simple
kitchen ware and the large vessels, used for the storage and transport
of loose and liquid produce (especially grain, wine and oil), to
ornamental vases (from the Latin *vas*, vessel), serving as votive gifts
for the gods and for the dead, as well as luxury articles in the homes of
the rich.

From the beginnings of pottery early in the Neolithic Age clay
vessels have provided the most frequently found evidence of human
habitation. Production techniques improved as civilization advanced,
pottery became more widely used and production soon became the
province of specialized craftsmen. Finds of pottery during archaeological excavations allow us to trace technical and cultural advances
in the different regions and at different times. It is thus possible to see
a continuity between sub-Mycenaean and Protogeometric pottery,
and to trace the impact of oriental influences on the Greek environment in the early archaic period. On the basis of specific features of
form and ornament it is then possible to establish a relative
chronology for periods for which a sufficient number of finds have
accumulated; this is a significant help in the dating of archaeological
strata and the definition of phases of artistic evolution. Pottery finds
allow us to form a picture of the extent and intensity of trade. We
have already seen the many ways in which pottery can be used as
source material for history.

In the seventh century the work of Corinthian potters dominated
the Greek scene. Elements assimilated from the east, primarily from
Phoenicia, are a marked feature of the ornament of Proto-Corinthian

vessels, a style which began to emerge in the last quarter of the eighth century BC. Lions, sphinxes and the mythical griffin were frequent motifs, but the Corinthian craftsmen did not simply imitate their models mechanically; their treatment of these oriental motifs was creative and original. In the second half of the seventh century human figures became more frequent in the decoration of vases. Besides Corinth itself, centres of pottery production were formed on Rhodes and on some of the Aegean islands, in Argos and in Laconia. As we have seen in the preceding chapter, Athens gradually came to the fore again, to occupy the dominating position which had been hers at the beginning of the archaic period, when the Geometric style was at its height. The Proto-Attic style gave rise to the black figure style at the beginning of the sixth century, followed by the red figure style. It is significant that most of the potters and vase painters who left their signatures on their work were from Athenian workshops. The only other pottery-producing centre which could compete with Athens on the level of artistic achievement in the second half of the sixth century was Chalcis.

Vase painting also provides an incomparable source of information on the life of archaic Greece. It gives an eloquent picture of the aristocratic way of life, a life of leisure spent in hunting and feasting, with dancers and music for entertainment; physical training and sports had their place, and military scenes are sometimes depicted on vases, but scenes from the life of shepherds and farmers, craftsmen, sailors or merchants, are rare. The painters portrayed the life they saw around them, although what they painted were mythological motifs, not scenes from real life. The Trojan myths were particularly popular, celebrating the deeds of the Achaean heroes, often with direct reference to Homer's epic. Another frequent source of inspiration were the legends woven around Heracles, Theseus and Perseus, illustrating not only stories of heroic ancestors endowed with superhuman strength and exceptional qualities, but man's eternal struggle with the forces of Nature and the malevolence of Fate. To make it easier to recognize the scenes painted on the vases, some artists added identity tags to their figures.

Part of pediment from the Old Temple of Athena
on the Athenian Acropolis, showing the three-bodied monster,
560–550 BC. Height of foremost figure 70.5cm (2ft 3¾in).
Acropolis Museum, Athens.

Above
Temple of Hera I (the 'Basilica') at Poseidonia (Paestum), about 530 BC.
Right
Detail of north frieze, which illustrates gigantomachy,
from the Siphnian treasury at Delphi, about 525 BC.
Height 64cm (2ft 1¼in). Delphi Museum.

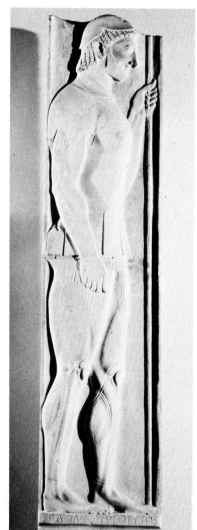

Above left
The Peplos Kore from the Acropolis in Athens,
about 540 BC. Marble. Height 120cm (3ft 11¼in).
Acropolis Museum, Athens.
Above right
Marble gravestone of Aristion (signed by the
artist Aristocles) from Velanideza, Attica, after 510 BC.
Height without base 240cm (7ft 10½in).
National Museum, Athens.

164

The Calf-Bearer from the Acropolis in Athens, 570 – 560 BC.
Marble. Height from the knees 96cm (3ft 1¾in).

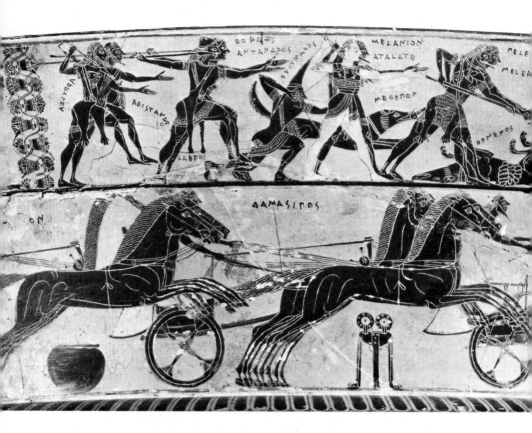

Above
Detail from the neck of the François Vase
— an Attic black figure volute krater from Chiusi, Etruria, signed by the potter
Ergotimos and the painter Kleitias — showing (above) the Calydonian boar
hunt and (below) chariots at the funeral games of Patroclus, about 570 BC.
Height of vase 66cm (2ft 2in). Museo Archeologico, Florence.
Above right
Attic black figure cup from Vulci, Etruria,
signed by the potter Exekias, showing Dionysus on a boat, about 530 BC.
Diameter 33cm (1ft 1in). Staatliche Antikensammlungen, Munich.
Right
Coin (tetradrachm) from Athens, showing head of Athena,
wearing crested Attic helmet, circular ear-ring and necklace, about 520–510 BC.
British Museum, London.

166

Above
Attic black figure cup from Vulci, Etruria, signed by
the potter Tleson, showing a hunter with hound and game,
about 550–540 BC. Diameter 7.6cm (3in). British Museum, London.

Top
Detail of a late Corinthian black figure column krater
from Caere, Etruria by the Three Maidens Painter, showing a wedding
procession, about 560 BC. Height of vase 42.5cm (1ft 4¾in).
Museo Etrusco Gregoriano, Vatican City.

The principal source for Greek mythology was Homeric poetry and the pantheon established in the *Iliad* and the *Odyssey* became the binding force of Greek culture. Mycenaean traditions and influences from the Near East merged here; the gods of Olympus have markedly anthropomorphic features, but they differ from human beings in being not only immortal, but also very powerful. In the *Iliad* the world of the gods shows marked features taken from the way of life of the tribal aristocracy, while in the *Odyssey* the social framework is broader, and moral values to be found in Hesiod already appear. According to Herodotus (2, 53) Hesiod and Homer 'gave the Greeks the lineage of the gods (*theogonien*) and gave the gods their epithets, distributed rank and the arts among them, and described their appearance'.

In his *Theogony* Hesiod, who seems to have become acquainted with the epics of Homer through wandering rhapsodists, established the systematic order of the Greek pantheon. His conception of three generations of gods based on the couples Uranus (the sky) and Gaia (the earth), Kronos and Rhea, Zeus and Hera, has been shown to have parallels in Hittite, Syrian and Babylonian literature. However, it is impossible to determine in what manner these motifs were assimilated. Hesiod may have been drawing on ancient Greek (Achaean) traditions which included elements originating in the Near East. The poet added ideas of his own, such as the view of the succeeding generations being as it were a preparation for the reign of Zeus. In the systematic genealogy set out in Hesiod's *Theogony* moral values have been given a place; for instance, Zeus and Themis (i.e. the given order, the symbol of justice) had three daughters called Eunomia ('good order'), Dike ('justice') and Eirene ('peace'). In this work, as in his *Labour and the Days*, Hesiod's gloomy view of the world shows through, but so does his faith in justice as dispensed by Zeus.

Among the poems dating from the archaic period there are also some dedicated to individual gods, which in classical times were attributed incorrectly to Homer. The Homeric hymn to Demeter, connected with the famous cult of the goddess at Eleusis, probably dates from shortly before the time when Eleusis became a part of Attica, that is to say in the seventh century. The hymn to Apollo was made up of two parts which were originally separate pieces; in one it is the god worshipped in the shrine on the island of Delos who is addressed, in the other it is the Delphic Apollo. In this hymn Apollo is not depicted as a feared archer whose wrath chastizes Agamemnon and the other Achaeans, as he is in the *Iliad*, but as a lyre-playing god, the patron of poetry. A hymn to Aphrodite, in which the goddess herself succumbs to her love for the Trojan hero Anchises, has an Ionian ambience; in it Aphrodite has features which are reminiscent of the ancient Asia Minor goddess of fertility. The latest of the surviving Homeric hymns is probably the one which tells of the fate of the young Hermes, written in a humorous mood which some- times verges on the comic. The Homeric hymns to Dionysus and Pan have only come down to us in fragments.

In the seventh and sixth centuries BC the lyric began to over- shadow epic poetry, and reached the height of its glory. It sprang from deep roots, for in Homeric epic we find references to song in honour of the gods, to nuptial song (*hymenaios*) and to lament (*threnos*) for fallen warriors. There are even references to songs sung at work. These songs came from folk tradition and folk poetry; like other peoples, the Greeks undoubtedly had a very ancient tradition of singing and dancing to the accompaniment of music.

The word lyric was not used until Hellenistic times, and comes from the fact that lyric verse was often sung or recited to the accompaniment of the lyre. In earlier times verse of this kind was called melic, i.e. song verse (*melos*, 'song'). Besides the lyre or other stringed instruments such as the *forminx* or *kitharis,* lyrics were often accompanied by the flute (*aulos*). In Greek tradition the lyre was regarded as a nobler and more refined instrument than the flute, which was especially popular at folk festivals connected with the worship of Dionysus.

During the archaic period Greek lyric poetry had already created several distinct forms differing both in subject matter and in metrical form. The closest to epic poetry was the elegy, which most probably evolved from the laments about fallen warriors sung by the Ionian Greeks in Asia Minor, influenced by their Lydian and Phrygian environment. It was composed in couplets made up of a dactylic hexameter and a pentameter, known as the short elegiac strophe. Elegies were soon broadened to include not only calls to battle, but also meditations on political and philosophical problems. The Ionian ambience also produced iambic verse, using the lively iambic trimeter and the calmer trochaic tetrameter. Iambic verse was particularly suitable for aggressive and polemical subjects, but such poems often came close to the elegy in their content. Monodic poetry, songs sung by one person, evolved in the Aeolian region, and particularly on the island of Lesbos; written in elegant metrical strophes, they usually expressed subjective feelings and moods. This was lyric poetry in the narrower sense of the word, and in character was closer to the modern lyric. The Dorian cities seem to have evolved choral lyric first. All these lyric forms preserved their traditional forms of expression, and especially their characteristic dialect, even when their authors came from other parts of the Greek world; even in classical times, in Attic drama, for example, the chorus was traditionally written in Dorian dialect.

The fact that lyric poetry flourished in the seventh and sixth centuries BC is a striking reflection of the profound changes Greek society was undergoing at that time. The evolution of the polis and the founding of colonies led to sharp social upheavals. The traditional bonds were slackened, and in the new conditions which emerged the creative force of imagination found an outlet and individual talent could make its mark. Literature shows similar trends to those which can be traced in the pictorial and plastic arts. Like many of the monuments of material culture, literature has only survived in fragmentary form. Archaic lyric poetry is known mainly from quotations found in later authors, supplemented by verses on Egyptian papyri of Hellenistic and Roman times. Most of the archaic poets themselves lived through stormy years of social stress, political conflict and military strife, and their verse serves as an authentic source of contemporary experience in the history of the different cities.

One of the founders of elegiac poetry was Callinus of Ephesus, who experienced the invasion of Asia Minor by nomad Cimmerians about the year 675 BC, when they dealt a fatal blow to the Phrygian kingdom and even looted the temple of Artemis in Ephesus. It is clear from the fragments of his verse which have survived that Callinus roused his fellow-citizens to fight for their country against the menace of enemy attack. Calls to valour are also the theme of Tyrtaeus in his verse, but he was urging the Spartans of the mid-seventh century to take arms against the uprising of the conquered people of neighbouring Messenia. Tyrtaeus followed in the tradition of Callinus not only in subject matter and metre, but in the use of the Ionian dialect as well. Suggestions that he came from Asia Minor were already being made in classical antiquity, but have been proved unfounded. The Ionian passages in the verse of this poet include obvious Doricisms.

Archilochus of Paros was a contemporary of Tyrtaeus; he wrote iambic and trochaic verse as well as elegies, and is considered the founder of the iambic lyric. His verse gives a vivid picture of the life of the soldier defending his country's interests in desperate struggles with the Thracians of the northern Aegean coast. He himself, however, was not only a warrior but a man who had felt 'the lovely gift of the Muses'. The fragments of his verse which have come down to us speak mainly of his love for Neobule, which was thwarted by her father Lycambes, who broke off their betrothal. The poet describes the sufferings of the balked lover and pours his hatred and scorn upon Lycambes. The poetry of Archilochus had many sides; he himself boasted that under the influence of wine he could compose a fine dithyramb in honour of Dionysus. He also wrote poems to other gods, as well as allegorical fables, sorrowful laments on the death of friends, and meditative verse on the ephemeral nature of human life. His poetry was a strong influence in the further development of Greek lyric poetry, and in later centuries remained a lively and unfailing source of inspiration.

The iambic verse written by Semonides of Amorgos was not

markedly original; he seems to have been somewhat younger than Archilochus, and his satire on the evil propensities of women, likening the different types of woman to animals or the elements of nature, was widely known in the ancient world. His ideal was the woman who, busy as a bee, looked after her family and beautified her husband's home. His parody tends to drop into banality. Phocylides of Miletus treated the same subject more briefly; his gnomes (or epigrams) in hexameter, were probably written at the beginning of the sixth century.

The elegies of Mimnermus of Colophon, at the end of the seventh and in the early sixth century, were rather sentimental. He sang the praises of the Greeks of Asia Minor and their heroism in the fighting against the Lydians, but above all he praised youth and love, lamenting over the sorrows of old age. His lines on the ephemeral nature of human life are sad and resigned, and his only desire is to die 'without heavy affliction and sickness' at the age of sixty.

Solon composed his verse in short elegiac strophes and in iambics and trochaics; he wrote not only of his public life and the urgent social problems of his native city, but of the problems common to all humanity. In the longest of his preserved poems, the elegy on the Muses, he hopes that he 'may always preserve a good reputation'. Asking the Muses to grant him riches he nevertheless — like Hesiod — does not want to acquire worldly wealth at whatever cost, quoting examples to illustrate the dangers attending all undertakings, and the capriciousness of fate. Other poems of his are expressions of the aristocratic ideal of pleasure in the hunt, in amusements and in sensual pleasures. In another poem that has survived Solon described the several phases of human life, which he gives as lasting seventy years. He also addressed lines to the poet Mimnermus, calling upon him to alter his wishes and try to attain the age of eighty. Unlike Archilochus with his pessimistic view of the fate of man after death, Solon hopes that his friends will mourn and sorrow at his death.

Hipponax of Ephesus fled from his native city when — probably soon after the middle of the sixth century — it was taken over by a tyrant under the auspices of the Persian king. He lived a life of poverty and want in Clazomenae, not far away, an unhappy exile. He liked the limping iambic foot (*choliambus*), which was well suited to the ironic mood of his verse. He ridiculed himself and his surroundings, and attacked his personal enemies mercilessly; a rough erotic note was not alien to his style, either. Lydian and Phrygian expressions found their way into his language.

The elegies of the Megarian poet Theognis are a valuable source of information for the social tensions in Megara towards the end of the archaic period. Nearly 1400 lines of verse attributed to him have survived, but only less than half can be considered authentic, while the rest were written later by different hands. Theognis was a militant protagonist of the aristocratic ideals, with which he also tried to inspire his beloved, Cyrnus; and he believed that his poems would be sung for ever at banquets, to the sound of the flute.

As we have seen in the chapter on the early history of Sparta, the poet Terpander from Antissa on Lesbos is said to have been there in the seventies of the seventh century. Classical tradition attributed to him the invention of the seven-stringed lyre. We know little of his poetry, but he appears to have been the founder of Aeolian melic poetry, which drew heavily on Lydian traditions. This type of lyric had attained masterly form on Lesbos at the turn of the seventh century, when the two greatest masters of monodic verse were writing there: Alcaeus and Sappho.

Alcaeus' verse was a call to arms in defence of the existing aristocratic order in his native Mytilene, but he did not sing only of battle — although we know from the troubled history of the city that he was active in the field. His drinking songs (*sympotika*) were an invitation to carefree revelry in the short days of winter and in the heat of summer. It is interesting to note that Alcaeus did not draw his inspiration solely from the life around him, but turned to literature as well, as we can see in his verses drawing directly on Hesiod; even here, of course, he treats Hesiod's theme in his own individual way

174

and his own style. He was a master of evocation, creating atmosphere in a few words. He also wrote poems on various mythical themes as well as hymns celebrating gods and heroes.

The poetry of Sappho, who was perhaps born at Eresus on Lesbos, was also closely bound up with the history of Mytilene, where she spent most of her life. We know her brother Charaxus as a merchant who traded with Naucratis in Egypt. While Alcaeus and the other aristocrats of Mytilene were preparing for battle and seeking solace in unbridled drinking bouts, Sappho lived among the maidens of Mytilene. She was perhaps the most successful of all the Greek poets in portraying the delights and the sufferings of love.

Her poems are hymns to physical and spiritual beauty, the feminine expression of the ideal of *kalokagathia*. She often speaks of her own feelings, convincingly portraying the ardour of passion, the torments of jealousy, sorrow at parting and longing for the beloved — and for her homeland, when (like Alcaeus) she was forced to leave Lesbos. Among the poems which have come down to us is a charming poem in which Sappho sings of the little daughter whom she would not exchange 'for the whole of Lydia'. She also wrote a number of wedding poems (*epithalamia*) rooted in ancient folk tradition, and a hymn to Hera and one to Aphrodite, which are among her most famous works.

The two lyric poets of Lesbos are usually grouped together with Anacreon of Teos, who lived in the second half of the sixth century. He left his native city as a young man, to escape the Persians, and settled first in Abdera on the Thracian coast. Like Archilochus before him, Anacreon took part in battles against the Thracians, and like the former, and his other poetic model, Alcaeus, he confessed to having thrown away his shield. Later he lived at the court of Polycrates on Samos, and in Athens under the rule of the sons of Peisistratus. The poetry of Anacreon is very varied. He could write lines attacking and ridiculing an arrogant newly-rich citizen, as effectively as he evoked in a few words the charm of a friendly gathering over a glass of wine and to the sound of song. Besides lyrics he wrote elegies, iambics and epigrams. His poems have neither the force of those of Alcaeus nor the depth of feeling of those of Sappho; they are calm and of great refinement. Like the verse of Theognis that of Anacreon was often imitated in classical antiquity.

Anonymous verse has also come down to us from the archaic period, especially the *scolia*, improvised verses which were a popular feature of banquets. For the most part they were mocking drinking songs, but at times they take on a political note, like the famous *scolia* celebrating the Athenian 'tyrannicides' Harmodius and Aristogeiton. We know some folk songs in honour of Spring, of the harvest, and of the potter's craft, and the epigrams preserved on clay vases and on gravestones are also anonymous.

At celebrations of a religious nature choral singing was the rule. Alcman, whom we have seen in Sparta in the middle of the seventh century, taking sides in the conflict between the people and the aristocrats, was believed to have been one of the originators of choral lyric singing. His songs for girls' choirs (*partheneia*) seem to have been part of the ritual in the temple of Artemis Orthia. Alcman is reputed for the masterly descriptions of the Greek countryside to be found in his poems.

Under the tyrant Periander, according to Herodotus (1, 23), the poet Arion composed dithyrambs in honour of Dionysus, in Corinth; he came from Methymna on the island of Lesbos. Stesichorus carried the choral lyric tradition still further. His work dates from the first half of the sixth century and is linked with Himera in Sicily. Only short fragments of the considerable works of Stesichorus have survived; he drew his inspiration from mythology, and from his own environment.

The poetry of Ibycus of Rhegium was strongly influenced by Stesichorus; his choral love songs date from the second half of the sixth century, when he spent some time at the court of Polycrates the tyrant of Samos, whom he celebrated in a poem. Like his predecessors he described the beauties of nature and sang the praises of love in a wealth of imagery which, however, lacks the personal feeling and the immediacy of the monodic lyric poetry.

The verse of Simonides of Ceos was simpler in style; he was born before the middle of the sixth century and lived to a great age. He spent some time in Athens under the sons of Peisistratus and again during the Persian Wars, and later lived on Sicily at the court of the tyrant of Syracuse, Hieron. He wrote laments (*threnoi*), hymns of praise (*enkomia*) and songs about the Olympic victors (*epinikia*). Most of his work falls into the fifth century, when his nephew Bacchylides was also writing choral songs. The Greek *epinikia* reached their apotheosis in the poems of Pindar.

The evolution of choral singing was connected with the beginnings of the drama, which — as is well known — reached its highest peak in the classical period. In Corinth Arion was writing dithyrambs, and a little later choral singing in honour of Dionysus was introduced at Sicyon, under the tyrant Cleisthenes. Under the tyranny of Peisistratus choruses in honour of Dionysus found fertile ground in Athens. According to classical tradition it was Thespis who added a story told by a narrator to the framework of choruses, thus laying the foundations of the dialogue between the actor and the leader of the chorus. The first tragedy is said to have been performed at the Great (City) Dionysia held during the sixty-first Olympiad (536/5 – 533/2 BC). The satyrs were an indispensable part of the worship of Dionysus; in the graphic and plastic arts they are usually depicted with horses' tails, but in the Peloponnese they were usually given the form of he-goats, which seems to have given rise to the Greek word *tragoidia* ('goat song'). Themes for the tragedies were drawn from mythology, and had nothing to do with the worship of Dionysus. The satyr plays developed alongside tragedy, with a chorus of satyrs providing comic and even burlesque effects. In archaic Athens Thespis was followed in the writing of tragedies by Choerilus and then Phrynichus; the latter's tragedy of the fall of Miletus, which was performed in 493/2 BC, a year after the disaster, is the first drama known to have been inspired by an important contemporary event.

Comedy also originated in the ceremonies connected with the worship of Dionysus, developing out of the ribald songs sung by tipsy revellers in the procession (*komos*). This kind of merriment was a popular form of entertainment among the ordinary people in many parts of Greece and in Greek colonies, but it was in fifth-century Attica that comedy evolved as a literary form. Performances were held at the Lenaea, festivals held in February at the very beginning of Spring, which were a celebration of the vegetative powers of nature.

Like the folk songs, folk tales were also handed down by oral tradition. Fables with a didactic aim, often of a social character, were very popular. Such tales were already known in the literature of Mesopotamia; there is a clever fox, for example, in the Sumerian Epic of Gilgamesh. In Greek poetry we have the fable of the nightingale and the hawk in Hesiod, and animals appearing in the work of Archilochus and Semonides. Aesopus (Aesop) was said by classical tradition to have collected an anthology of prose fables. Herodotus tells us (2, 134) that Aesop was a slave living on Samos about the middle of the sixth century BC. So many legends accrued to the figure of Aesop even in antiquity that the historical reality has almost disappeared. As far as is known, the collection of fables dates from as late as the end of the fourth century BC, but all that has survived are verse renderings dating from Imperial Rome, and prose versions by Byzantine authors.

In addition to fables there were, especially in Ionian regions, romances, one of which was the story (*logos*) of the trials of King Croesus of Lydia, recorded by Herodotus in the first book of his *History*. By the end of the archaic period the figure of this powerful but later sadly chastised ruler seems to have been linked with the story of the great thinkers who were called the Seven Sages (*sophoi*) in the Greek tradition. The seven wise men already appeared in the Epic of Gilgamesh, but in Sumerian mythology they were good spirits who fought against the same number of evil demons. In the Greek version the Seven Sages included men who were historical figures in early Greece, although they were shrouded in legend; statements, and later even letters, were invented and attributed to them. The names of the seven are not agreed on by all ancient authors. Among the standard figures of the seven was the Athenian poet and statesman

Solon; the *aesymnetes* of Mytilene, Pittacus; Bias of Priene in Asia Minor; and Thales of neighbouring Miletus. Among the remaining, the most frequently named are the Corinthian tyrant Periander, Cleobulus the tyrant of Lindos on Rhodes, and Chilon the Spartan ephor.

After Solon, the most remarkable of the Seven Sages was Thales, the founder of the first school of philosophy in Greek thought. His reputation was made when he predicted the eclipse of the sun which took place during a battle between the Medes and the Lydians on May 28th 585 BC. He drew his mathematical and astronomical knowledge from the Egyptians and Babylonians, and under the influence of oriental cosmogonies he was able to rid his thought of the accepted ideas of Greek epic poetry. He believed that the earth floats on water, seeing in water the living matter from which all else has been created. His materialist view of the origin and nature of the world nevertheless included the belief that there were gods everywhere.

Anaximander, the disciple of Thales, carried his ideas further. A number of discoveries in the natural sciences are attributed to him, particularly in astronomy. One of his remarkable ideas was that the world was formed from a ball of fire which broke into circles, which then became the sun, moon and stars. He believed that the earth was floating free, maintaining its position because it was at the same distance from all points. Anaximander was in advance of his time, too, in his theory that life originated in water, and that man had evolved from other animal species. He thought the primeval substance was *apeiron* (the unlimited infinite), and declared that objects come into being as the result of perpetual motion, in the course of which contrary substances are discharged.

The third of the philosophers of Miletus was Anaximenes, who died during the sixty-third Olympiad, i.e. between 528 and 525 BC. He believed that the primeval substance was the air, which he thought identical with god. All other substances evolved through the condensation or dilution of the air, which is permanently in motion. The earth, the sun, the moon and the other heavenly bodies, which are of fire, are floating in the air, which is limitless. The stars do not give off heat because they are too far away. Anaximenes' ideas reveal a greater measure of experimental work than those of his predecessors.

Side by side with a rationalist approach to the question of the origin and development of the world, teachings of a mystical nature were widespread. The Greeks assimilated not only knowledge of the nature of the physical world and its laws, but also various mythical and religious ideas from their eastern neighbours. Orphism was particularly popular in archaic Greece; the cult was thought to have orginated with the mythical Thracian singer, Orpheus. One of the most marked features of Orphism was the belief that the human soul is part of the divine and therefore immortal. In contrast to the evolutionary theogony of Hesiod, the Orphics taught that Zeus was the eternal god, 'first born and the last to be'. One of the Orphic thinkers was Epimenides of Crete, who was traditionally said to have cleansed Athens of the stain of the murder of the followers of Cylon; he sometimes appeared as one of the Seven Sages. Pherecydes of Syros wrote a prose version of the cosmogony of the Orphics, in the middle of the sixth century, and fragments have survived in the works of later authors. According to Pherecydes, Zas (Zeus), Kronos (identified with Chronos, the god of time), and Chthonia (earthly, the goddess of the earth), were all eternal. Zeus, taking upon himself the form of Eros, created the earth and gave all things unity. The human soul is immortal, and is purged of sin after the death of the body by incarnation in another living creature. The Athenian soothsayer Onomacritus, who lived during the tyranny of the sons of Peisistratus, was an Orphic. Orphism was very popular among Greek colonists in Sicily and southern Italy.

There are Orphic elements in the thought of some of the idealistic philosophers, particularly the followers of Pythagoras. Born on Samos, Pythagoras left when the tyrant Polycrates came to power, and settled in southern Italy. He taught in Croton, and died in Metapontum. He led his followers to foster the intellect, which he saw as the way to spiritual purification; because he believed in the transmigration of souls, he deprecated the eating of meat. His theory of the order of the natural world assigned an important place to numerical relations; although the famous theorem which bears his name, and states that the square on the hypotenuse of a right-angled triangle is equal to the sum of the squares on the other two sides, was already known before his time, Pythagoras devoted himself to the study of mathematics and the other natural sciences, and established the numerical relations of the musical scale. He believed that the ideal state of the world was one of harmony, and that it could be achieved by maintaining the proper proportions in all things, and balancing opposites. Pythagoras enjoyed great authority among his disciples and followers, and his successors often quoted him in support of their theories, although the words attributed to him are not always authentic. One of the early Pythagoreans was Alcmeon of Croton, who gained valuable insights particularly into medical science, at the turn of the sixth century. He realized that all sensory perception becomes reality only through the brain, and was the first to dare to dissect the human body.

Xenophanes of Colophon, who fled from his native city about 540 BC, to escape the Persians, was active in southern Italy at the same time as Pythagoras; he lived in Hyele (Elea), and his thought is known primarily from his verse. Xenophanes was highly critical of the gods as depicted by Homer and Hesiod, and commented iron-ically that if the animals were able to create gods for themselves 'the gods of the horses would resemble horses and those of the oxen would resemble oxen' (13, 1–2; Diehl). He believed that 'between the gods and men' there was but one supreme omniscient god who bore no resemblance whatever to mortal creatures and stayed immobile in the same place. Unlike the Milesian philosophers, who stressed motion and the changing nature of things, Xenophanes laid greatest emphasis on the immutability and infinite duration of the world. These ideas were taken up by Parmenides, who is sometimes regarded as the real founder of the Eleatic school of philosophy. He tried to prove that the only true reality is being (*to on*), which has neither been created nor will it pass, and therefore has neither past nor future; it is constant and indivisible. He attacked the contemporary philosophy in his verse, meaning perhaps Heraclitus.

Heraclitus of Ephesus was one of the most original thinkers of ancient Greece. Of an ancient aristocratic family, he is said to have given up the privileges he enjoyed by right of birth, and devoted himself to philosophy. Like Parmenides he was at the height of his powers at about 500 BC. Numerous fragments of his works have come down to us; he was critical of the Greek poets (Homer, Hesiod and Archilochus) and of the philosophers (Xenophanes, and especially Pythagoras), and set forth his own ideas in language rich in imagery and similes. He was already considered an 'obscure' philosopher in antiquity. He drew on the ideas of the Milesian school, but for him fire was not only the primeval substance of the world, but also the divine principle, called by him *logos* ('word', 'thought', 'reason'). All other substances are exchanged for fire just as goods are exchanged for gold. Heraclitus believed that the most important factor in all things in nature and in human society was war [struggle], which is 'father and king of all things', and motion, which leads to constant change. Thus 'we go down into the same rivers, yet we do not, we are and yet we are not'. All matter is in constant flux, and harmony is achieved by the balance of opposites. Heraclitus expressed the dialectical unity of the world in the famous declaration that 'this world which is the same for all, was not created by any god nor by men, but always was, is and will always be an ever-living fire, kindling and dying down according to its measure.'

The Greek thinkers not only studied natural phenomena to determine natural laws, but tried to distinguish laws in the relationships between human beings. We have already seen how the poets and philosophers of antiquity often meditated on the nature and ordering of society. The desire to explore far-away lands, together with the expansion of colonization, led to developments in geography, ethnography, and historiography. Scylax of Caryanda, in the service of Darius of Persia, sailed up the river Indus and into the Indian Ocean and the Red Sea, and described his experiences in a book which has not survived, but was one of the first Greek travel books. At the same period Hecataeus of Miletus wrote a systematic description of the world as then known, and like his fellow-country-man and teacher, Anaximander, Hecataeus put together a geographical map. He was also the author of a historiographical work which we find Herodotus drawing on.

The archaic period thus saw the foundations laid for philosophy and many branches of science and humanities. Greek thinkers drew on the experience accumulated for many centuries by the scholars of Babylonia and Egypt before them, but they were not so much concerned with the practical application of the knowledge thus acquired as with its significance for the solution of general questions concerning the nature of the world. The great difference in their approach was due to the fact that the Greek philosophers, mathematicians and historians were citizens of a city-state (polis) and were able to develop their individual personalities without constraint; in their environment it was possible to pose questions freely which would overturn the traditionally held views of nature and human society. There were similar tendencies in poetry and art, as well as in the sciences.

During the first half of the first millennium BC the Greeks not only overcame the consequences of political upheaval and the economic stagnation of the 'Dark Ages', but entered upon a new historical epoch to which we give the name of classical antiquity. Greek civilization rose on the ruins of the Cretan-Mycenaean civilization, and in many respects carried on its traditions. The Greeks also drew on the rich heritage of the civilizations of the ancient Near East, for this was the broader context in which they lived. And they were in contact with many other regions, in the Mediterranean and the Black Sea, which were also a source of stimulus and experience.

These very varied influences were nevertheless no threat to the specific characteristic features of Greek civilization in the socio-economic structure or in the political and cultural spheres. The Greek polis which — according to Aristotle's definition — was 'a community of the free', enabled its citizens to develop their talents freely; at the same time the slaves and the other subject population were severely oppressed, and there was social inequality even within the citizen body. Nevertheless the emergence of the city-state was an important step forward in social development.

At the very beginning of the fifth century BC Greek civilization proved its strength and powers of resistance in the conflict with the Persian Empire which is rightly regarded as the turning point between the archaic and the classical periods of Greek history. It was not only a matter of military victory over a much more powerful enemy; as it developed further Greek civilization proved its superiority and viability in the success it achieved in all spheres of human knowledge and activity, and became one of the most influential forces in the history of the ancient world.

Maps

Greece, Crete and the Aegean area to the sixth century BC

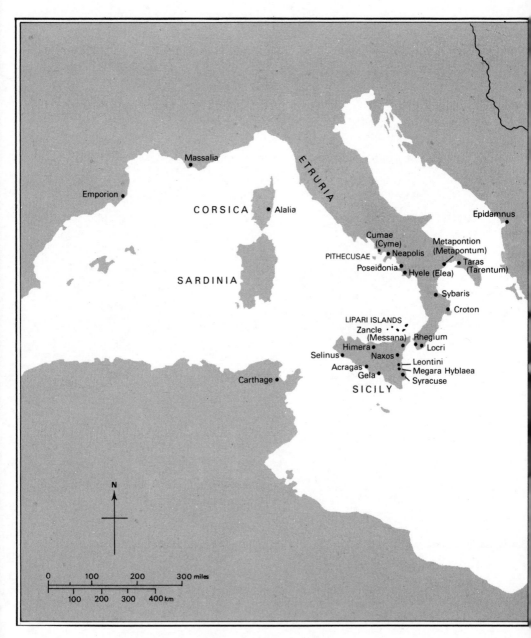

The Mediterranean and the Black Sea showing Greek colonies from the
eighth to the sixth century BC

186

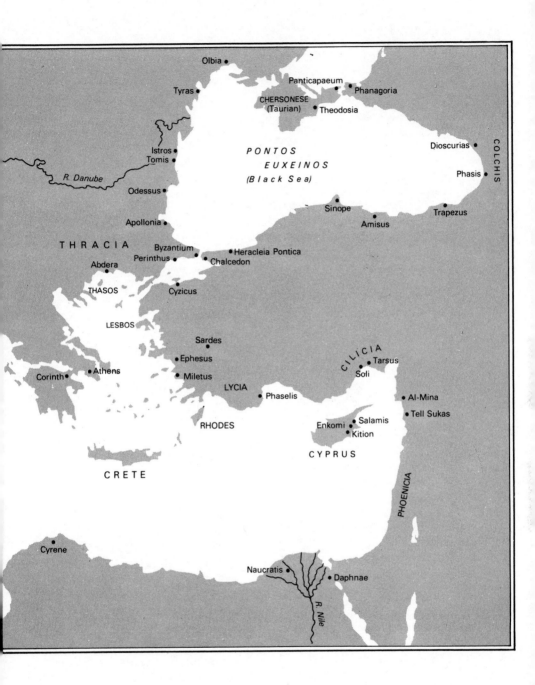

Olbia •

Panticapaeum
• Tyras •   • Phanagoria
CHERSONESE   • Theodosia
(Taurian)

Istros •   *P O N T O S*   COLCHIS
Tomis •   *E U X E I N O S*   Dioscurias •
R. Danube   *(Black Sea)*   Phasis •

Odessus •   • Trapezus
                    Sinope •
Apollonia •   Amisus •

T H R A C I A   Byzantium
Abdera   Perinthus • • Heracleia Pontica
THASOS   • Chalcedon
          • Cyzicus
LESBOS

            Sardes •   C I L I C I A
         • Ephesus   • Tarsus
Corinth • • Athens • Miletus   Soli •
              LYCIA   • Al-Mina
                 • Phaselis   • Tell Sukas
RHODES   Enkomi • • Salamis
                    • Kition
C R E T E   C Y P R U S

                                    PHOENICIA

Cyrene •
           Naucratis • • Daphnae
                    R. Nile

187

Bibliography

E.Akurgal *The Art of Greece: Its
Origins in the Mediterranean and the
Near East* New York 1968

A.Andrewes *The Greek Tyrants*
London 1956

A.Andrewes *The Greeks* London 1967

M.Andronicos *Herakleion Museum and
Archaeological Sites of Crete* Athens
1975

M.T.W. Arnheim *Aristocracy in Greek
Society* London 1977

M.Austin *Greece and Egypt in the
Archaic Age* Cambridge 1970

J.D.Beazley *Attic Black-Figure Vase-
Painters* Oxford 1956

J.D.Beazley *Attic Red-Figure Vase-
Painters* Oxford 1963

J.D.Beazley *The Development of Attic
Black-Figure* Berkeley 1964

H.Bengtson *Griechische Geschichte*
Munich 1977

J.L.Benson *Horse, Bird and Man: The
Origins of Greek Painting* Amherst,
Mass. 1970

J.Bérard *La colonization grecque de
l'Italie méridionale et la Sicile dans
l'Antiquité: l'histoire et la légende*
Paris 1957

J.Bérard *L'expansion et la colonisation
grecque jusqu'aux guerres médiques*
Paris 1960

B.Bergquist *The Archaic Greek
Temenos: A Study of Structure and
Function* Lund 1967

H.Berve *Die Tyrannis bei den Griechen*
Munich 1967

T.V.Blavatskaya *Akheyskaya Gretsiya*
('Achaean Greece') Moscow 1966

C.W.Blegen *Troy* London 1963

J.Boardman *Archaic Greek Gems*
Evanston and London 1968

J.Boardman *Athenian Black Figure
Vases* London 1974; New York
1975

J.Boardman *Athenian Red Figure Vases
of the Archaic Period* London 1975

J.Boardman *Greek Art* London 1964;
New York 1973

J.Boardman *The Greeks Overseas*
Harmondsworth 1973

J.Boardman *Greek Sculpture: The
Archaic Period* London and New
York 1978

B.Borecký *Survivals of Some Tribal
Ideas in Classical Greek* Prague 1965

J.Bouzek *Homerisches Griechenland im
Lichte der archäologischen Quellen*
Prague 1969

C.M.Bowra *Greek Lyric Poetry from
Alcman to Simonides* Oxford 1961

C.M.Bowra *Homer and his Forerunners*
Edinburgh 1955

A.R.Burn *The Lyric Age of Greece*
London 1960

A.R.Burn *Persia and the Greeks*
London and New York 1962

A.R.Burn *The Warring States of
Greece* London 1968

C.Calame *Les choeurs de jeunes filles en
Grèce archaïque I&II* Urbino and
Rome 1977

R.Carpenter *Discontinuity in Greek Civilization* Cambridge 1966

P.Cartledge *Sparta and Lakonia* London and Boston 1979

J.L. Caskey, 'Greece, Crete and the Aegean Islands in the Early Bronze Age' in *Cambridge Ancient History* Vol. I Pt 2, 1971

J.L.Caskey, 'Greece and the Aegean Islands in the Middle Bronze Age' in *Cambridge Ancient History* Vol. II Pt 1, 1973

L.Casson *Ships and Seamanship in the Ancient World* Princeton 1971

J.Chadwick *The Decipherment of Linear B* Cambridge 1958

J.Chadwick *The Mycenaean World* Cambridge 1966

F.Chamoux *La civilisation grecque* Paris 1963

J.Charbonneaux, R. Martin and F. Villard *Archaic Greek Art, 620–480 B.C.* London and New York 1971

J.N.Coldstream *Greek Geometric Pottery* London 1968

J.M.Cook *The Greeks in Ionia and the East* London 1962

R.A.Crossland, 'Immigrants from the North' in *Cambridge Ancient History* Vol. I Pt 2, 1971

R.A.Crossland and A. Birchall (Ed.) *Bronze Age Migrations in the Aegean* London 1974

P.Demargne *Aegean Art: The Origins of Greek Art* London 1964

V.R.d'A. Desborough *The Greek Dark Ages* London 1972

V.R.d'A. Desborough *The Last Mycenaeans and their Successors* Oxford 1964

V.R.d'A. Desborough *Protogeometric Pottery* Oxford 1952

B.C.Dietrich *The Origins of Greek Religion* Berlin and New York 1974

T.J.Dunbabin *The Greeks and their Eastern Neighbours* London 1957

T.J.Dunbabin *The Western Greeks* Oxford 1948

V.Ehrenberg *Aspects of the Ancient World* Oxford 1946

V.Ehrenberg *The Greek State* London 1969

V.Ehrenberg *Neugründer des Staates* Munich 1925

V.Ehrenberg *Die Rechtsidee im frühen Griechentum* Leipzig 1921 (reprint, Darmstadt 1966)

V.Ehrenberg *From Solon to Socrates* London 1973

G.F.Else *The Origin and Early Form of Greek Tragedy* Cambridge, Mass. 1965

G.Ferrara *La politica di Solone* Naples 1964

M.I.Finley *Early Greece: The Bronze and Archaic Ages* London 1970

M.I.Finley *The History of Sicily: Ancient Sicily to the Arab Conquest* London 1968

M.I.Finley *The World of Odysseus* revised edition, New York 1965 and Harmondsworth 1967

W.G.Forrest *The Emergence of Greek Democracy* London 1966

W.G.Forrest *A History of Sparta, 950–192 B.C.* London 1968

H.Fränkel *Dichtung und Philosophie des frühen Griechentums* Munich 1969

K.Freeman *The Work and Life of Solon* Cardiff 1926

A.French *The Growth of the Athenian Economy* London 1964

A.G.Galanopoulos and E.Bacon *Atlantis: The Truth behind the Legend* London 1969

F.Ghinatti *I gruppi politici ateniesi fino alle guerre persiane* Rome 1970

O.Gigon *Grundprobleme der antiken Philosophie* Berne 1959

A.J.Graham *Colony and Mother City in Ancient Greece* Manchester 1964

J.W.Graham *The Palaces of Crete* Princeton 1962

P.A.L.Greenhalgh *Early Greek Warfare* Cambridge 1973

G.Hafner *Art of Crete, Mycenae, and Greece* New York and London 1968

N.G.L. Hammond *History of the Hellenic World: The Archaic Period* Athens and London 1975

N.G.L.Hammond *History of the Hellenic World: Prehistory and Protohistory* Athens 1974

N.G.L.Hammond *Migrations and Invasions in Greece and Adjacent Areas* New Jersey 1976

J.Hawkes *Dawn of the Gods: Minoan and Mycenaean Origins of Greece* New York 1968

J.Hejnic *Pausanias the Perieget and the Archaic History of Arcadia* Prague 1961

R.Higgins *Minoan and Mycenaean Art* London 1967

N.Himmelmann *Archäologisches zum Problem der griechischen Sklaverei* Wiesbaden 1971

N.Himmelmann *Über die bildende Kunst in der homerischen Gesellschaft* Mainz 1969

S.Hood *The Home of the Heroes: The Aegean before the Greeks* London and New York 1967

S.Hood *The Minoans* London 1971

J.T.Hooker *The Ancient Spartans* London, Toronto and Melbourne 1980

J.T.Hooker *Mycenaean Greece* London 1976

R.Hope Simpson *A Gazetteer and Atlas of Mycenaean Sites* London 1965

R.J.Hopper *The Early Greeks* London 1976

R.W.Hutchinson *Prehistoric Crete* Harmondsworth 1962

G.L.Huxley *Achaeans and the Hittites* Belfast 1964

G.L.Huxley *The Early Ionians* London 1966

G.L.Huxley *Early Sparta* London 1962

G.Isler-Kerényi *Nike. Der Typus der laufenden Flügelfrau in archaischer Zeit* Erlenbach and Zurich 1969

F.Jacoby *Atthis* Oxford 1949

W.Jaeger *Paideia I* Oxford 1939

P.Janni *La cultura di Sparta arcaica, Ricerche I* Rome 1965, *Ricerche II* Rome 1970

L.H.Jeffery *Archaic Greece: The City-States, c.700 – 500 B.C.* New York 1976

L.H.Jeffery *The Local Scripts of Archaic Greece* Oxford 1961

A.Johnston *The Emergence of Greece* Oxford 1976

A.H.M.Jones *Sparta* Oxford 1967

P.P.Kahane *Ancient and Classical Art* London 1969

T.Kelly *A History of Argos to 500 B.C.* Minneapolis 1976

F.Ch.Kessidi *Ot mifa k logosu* ('From Myth to Logos') Moscow 1972

F.Kiechle *Lakonien and Sparta* Munich 1963

F.Kiechle *Messenische Studien* Munich 1957

K.H.Kinzl (Ed.) *Die ältere Tyrannis bis zu den Perserkriegen* Darmstadt 1979

J.Kleine *Untersuchungen zur Chronologie der attischen Kunst von*

Peisistratos bis Themistokles
Tübingen 1973

G.Kleiner *Alt-Milet* Wiesbaden 1966

C.M.Kraay and M.Hirmer *Greek Coins* London 1966

F.Krauss *Die Tempel von Paestum I: Der Athenatempel* Berlin 1959

P.de La Coste-Messelière *Au musée de Delphes: recherches sur quelques monuments archaïque et leur décor sculpté* Paris 1936

E.Langlotz *Frühgriechische Bildhauerschulen* Nuremberg 1927

V.V.Lapin *Grecheskaya kolonizatsiya Severnovo Prichernomorya* ('Greek Colonization on the North Shores of the Black Sea') Kiev 1966

J.A.Lencman *Die Sklaverei im mykenischen und homerischen Griechenland* Wiesbaden 1966

A.Lesky *A History of Greek Literature* London 1966

P.Lévêque and P.Vidal-Naquet *Clisthène l'Athénien* Besançon and Paris 1973

D.Lotze *Metaxy eleutheron kai doulon* Berlin 1959

S.J Luria *Yazyk i kultura mikenskoy Gretsiyi* ('Language and Culture of the Mycenaean Greece') Moscow and Leningrad 1957

S.Marinatos and M.Hirmer *Crete and Mycenae* London 1960

A.Masaracchia *Solone* Florence 1958

F.Matz *Geschichte der griechischen Kunst I: Die geometrische und die früharchaische Form* Frankfurt (Main) 1950

F.Matz *Kreta und frühes Griechenland* Baden-Baden 1965

S.Mazzarino *Fra Oriente e Occidente: Ricerche di storia greca arcaica* Florence 1947

J.Mellaart *The Archaeology of Ancient Turkey* London, Sydney and Toronto 1978

H.Michell *Sparta* Cambridge 1952

S.Miller *Studies in Chronology I & II* Albany 1970–1971

S.Moscati *The World of the Phoenicians* London 1968

G.E.Mylonas *The Cult Center of Mycenae* Athens 1972

G.E.Mylonas *Mycenae and the Mycenaean Age* Princeton 1968

M.P.Nilsson *The Minoan-Mycenaean Religion and its Survival in Greek Religion* Lund 1950

I.G.Nixon *The Rise of the Dorians* Cambridge 1968

P.Oliva *Raná řecká tyrannis* ('Early Greek Tyranny') Prague 1954

P.Oliva *Solón* Prague 1971

P.Oliva *Sparta and her Social Problems* Prague and Amsterdam 1971

D.L.Page *History and the Homeric Iliad* Berkeley and Los Angeles 1959

D.L.Page *The Santorini Volcano and the Destruction of Minoan Crete* London 1970

L.R.Palmer *The Interpretation of Mycenaean Greek Texts* Oxford 1963

L.R.Palmer *Mycenaeans and Minoans: Aegean Prehistory in the Light of the Linear B Tablets* London 1961

A.W.Pickard-Cambridge *The Dramatic Festivals of Athens* Oxford 1953

R.Pleiner *Iron Working in Ancient Greece* Prague 1968

M.J.Price and N.Waggoner *Archaic Greek Coinage* London 1976

A.E.Raubitschek *Dedications from the Athenian Acropolis: A Catalogue of Inscriptions of the Sixth and Fifth Centuries B.C.* (edited with the collaboration of L.H.Jeffery) Cambridge, Mass. 1949

C.Renfrew *The Emergence of Civilization* London 1972

O.Reuther *Der Heratempel von Samos: Der Bau der Zeit des Polykrates* Berlin 1957

G.M.A.Richter *The Archaic Gravestones of Attica* London 1961

G.M.A.Richter *Archaic Greek Art against its Historical Background* New York and Oxford 1949

G.M.A.Richter *Korai: Archaic Greek Maidens* London 1968

G.M.A.Richter *Kouroi. Archaic Greek Youths* London 1970

G.M.A.Richter *The Portraits of the Greeks, I* London 1965

B.S.Ridgway *The Archaic Style in Greek Sculpture* Princeton 1977

C.Roebuck *Ionian Trade and Colonization* New York 1959

D.Roussel *Tribu et cité* Besançon and Paris 1976

P.Roussel *Sparte* Paris 1960

E.Ruschenbusch *Solonos nomoi* Wiesbaden 1966

M.B.Sakellariou *La migration grecque en Ionie* Athens 1958

A.E.Samuel *The Mycenaeans in History* Englewood Cliffs, NJ 1966

N.K.Sandars *The Sea Peoples: Warriors of the Ancient Mediterranean, 1250–1150 B.C.* London 1978

F.Schachermeyr *Die ägäische Frühzeit,I:Die vormykenischen Perioden des griechischen Festlandes und der Kykladen* Vienna 1976

F.Schachermeyr *Die ältesten Kulturen Griechenlands* Stuttgart 1955

F.Schachermeyr *Die minoische Kultur des alten Kreta* Stuttgart 1964

K.Schefold *Myth and Legend in Early Greek Art* London 1966

L.A.Schneider *Zur sozialen Bedeutung der archaischen Korenstatuen* Hamburg 1975

B.Schweitzer *Die geometrische Kunst Griechenlands* Cologne 1969

E.Simon *Die griechischen Vasen* Munich 1976

B.Snell *Die Entdeckung des Geistes* Hamburg 1955

B.Snell *Leben und Meinungen der Sieben Weisen* Munich 1952

A.M.Snodgrass *The Dark Age of Greece* Edinburgh 1971

A.M.Snodgrass *Early Greek Armour and Weapons from the End of the Bronze Age to 600 B.C.* Edinburgh 1964

G.Sokolov *Egeyskoye iskusstvo* ('Aegean Art') Moscow 1972

P.Spahn *Mittelschicht und Polisbildung* Frankfurt (Main), Berne and Las Vegas 1977

C.G.Starr *The Economic and Social Growth of Early Greece, 800–500 B.C.* New York and Oxford 1977

C.G.Starr *The Origins of Greek Civilization, 1100–650 B.C.* New York 1961

L.A.Stella *Tradizione micenea e poesia dell'Iliade* Rome 1978

C.M.Stibbe *Lakonische Vasenmaler des sechsten Jahrhunderts vor Christus* Amsterdam 1972

H.E.Stier *Die geschichtliche Bedeutung des Hellenennamens* Cologne 1970

D.E.Strong *The Classical World* London 1965

R.S.Stroud *Drakon's Law on Homicide* Berkeley 1968

F.M.Stubbings, 'The Aegean Bronze Age' in *Cambridge Ancient History* Vol. I Pt 1, 1970

F.M.Stubbings, 'The Expansion of Mycenaean Civilization' in

Cambridge Ancient History Vol. II Pt 1, 1973

F.M.Stubbings, 'The Rise of Mycenaean Civilization', in *Cambridge Ancient History* Vol. II Pt 1, 1973

C.G.Styrenius *Submycenaean Studies* Lund 1967

W.Taylour *The Mycenaeans* London 1964

G.Thomson *Aeschylus and Athens* London 1946

G.Thomson *Studies in Ancient Greek Society, I: The Prehistoric Aegean* London 1954, *II: The First Philosophers* London 1955

V.S.Titov *Neolit Gretsiyi* (The Neolithic Period in Greece) Moscow 1969

A.J.Toynbee *Some Problems of Greek History* London 1969

P.N.Ure *The Origin of Tyranny* Cambridge 1922

G.Vallet *Rhégion et Zancle: Histoire, commerce et civilization des cités chalcidiennes du dédroit de Messine* Paris 1958

M.Ventris and J.Chadwick *Documents in Mycenaean Greek* Cambridge 1973

E.Vermeule *Greece in the Bronze Age* Chicago 1964

J.-P.Vernant *Mythe et pensée chez les Grecs* Paris 1965

J.-P.Vernant *Mythe et société en Grèce ancienne* Paris 1974

J.-P.Vernant *Les origines de la pensée grecque* Paris 1962

F.Villard *Sicile grecque* Paris 1955

F.Villard *Les vases grecs* Paris 1956

H.T.Wade-Gery *Essays in Greek History* Oxford 1958

K.Wallenstein *Korinthische Plastik des siebenten und sechsten Jahrhunderts vor Christus* Bonn 1971

T.B.L.Webster *From Mycenae to Homer* London 1958

H.Weigel *Der Troianische Krieg: Die Lösung* Darmstadt 1970

S.S.Weinberg, 'The Stone Age in the Aegean' in *Cambridge Ancient History* Vol. I Pt 1, 1970

M.L.West *Early Greek Philosophy and the Orient* Oxford 1971

E.Will *Doriens et Ioniens: Essai sur la valeur du critère ethnique appliqué à l'étude d'histoire et de la civilisation grecque* Paris 1956

E.Will *Korinthiaka. Recherches sur l'histoire et la civilisation de Corinthe des origines aux guerres médiques* Paris 1955

R.F.Willetts *Ancient Crete: A Social History* London and Toronto 1966

R.F.Willetts *Aristocratic Society in Ancient Crete* London 1955

R.F.Willetts *The Civilization of Ancient Crete* London 1977

A.G.Woodhead *The Greeks in the West* London 1962

W.J.Woodhouse *Solon the Liberator* Oxford 1938 (reprint, New York 1965)

K.K.Zelyin *Borba politicheskikh gruppirovok v Attike v VI veke do n.e.* ('The Struggle of the Political Groups in Attica during the sixth century B.C.') Moscow 1964

Index

Page numbers in italics refer to illustrations.

194